MIKE SIMMONS

TAKE THE HIGH ROAD

DOING THE RIGHT THING

CHRISTIANOLOGY SERIES

ALL SCRIPTURE IS THE KING JAMES VERSION OF THE BIBLE

Christianology Publications

Copyright 2021 Christianology Publications

No part of this publication may be reproduced or copied in any form without written permission from the copyright owner.

ISBN 978-0-578-64440-0

TABLE OF CONTENTS

1. Are Christians Accountable for their Actions?
2. Trying to do the Right Thing Goes Nowhere Without God
3. You are Considered Valuable to Heaven
4. Intentions
5. When the Devil is Camped Outside Your Door
6. Who Shall Deliver Me?
7. DO NOT LUST
8. Our Rock of Offence
9. How is Your Speech?
10. The Sin of Unbelief
11. The High Cost of Low Living
12. The Sin of Indifference

Introduction

We all have choices to make in life which will affect the outcome of our future. The right decisions can lead us down the path of righteousness that God can lead and use for his glory. When we make the wrong decisions and take the road most traveled by the world, it can lead to disaster, tragedy, and remorse.

Temptations always bring the Christian to a crossroads to make a decision on which way to go. Taking the high road means that you have chosen to not let the flesh win and decide to be spiritual.

"For to be carnally minded is death: but to be spiritually minded is life and peace. Because the carnal mind is enmity against God: for it is not subject to the law of God, neither indeed can be. So then they that are in the flesh cannot please God." Romans 8: 6-8

When you have settled on your own decisions for your life, where has it gotten you so far? Are you stuck in a comfort zone and not seeing any real blessings from God? Yield yourself to the Holy Spirit and accept new challenges that only faith can bring. It is easy to see that you may have made the wrong choices and resent yourself to some degree, but it is never too late to take the high road and change your entire life and future.

Take the High Road
Doing the Right Thing

Chapter One

Are Christians Accountable for Their Actions?

Actions Speak Out and Make Lasting Impressions.

Many believers today find comfort in knowing that they are saved, therefore safe from any consequences of sin. The truth is that God loves us just the way we are, but too much to leave us that way.

The influence of Christianity is made void when one sins, and people will not take you seriously or they feel they don't want any part of that lifestyle. Actions speak louder than words.

In I Corinthians 6:9-12, the Bible tells us, "Know ye not that the unrighteous shall not inherit the kingdom of God? Be not deceived: neither fornicators, nor idolaters, nor adulterers, nor effeminate, nor abusers of themselves with mankind, nor thieves, nor covetous, nor drunkards, nor revilers, nor extortioners, shall inherit the kingdom of God. And such were some of you: but ye are washed, but ye are sanctified, but ye are justified in the name of the Lord Jesus, and by the Spirit of our God. All things are lawful unto me, but all things are not expedient: all things are lawful for me, but I will not be brought under the power of any." The power of the flesh can make you lose sight of who you are.

Beware, lasting impressions are difficult to erase in people's minds. Once you have made a memory for someone, they will always connect you with that action. For example, a young man received a .22 rifle for Christmas and loved to go hunting small game. He noticed one day that his gun was missing out of the closet where he always kept it. Nobody knew anything about the whereabouts of the missing rifle, but someone had to know the truth. Years went by and still no answers. One day after watching a relative pawn off some valuables to fund his alcoholic lifestyle, he remembered the look on his face when asked if he knew anything. Did that relative pawn that .22 rifle to buy liquor? This suspicion always stuck in the mind of when he saw that relative. He never forgot.

Would a Christian stoop so low as to steal from another, or would a Christian cheat on their spouse or girlfriend/boyfriend? "For none of us liveth to himself, and no man dieth to himself. For whether we live, we live unto the Lord; and whether we die, we die unto the Lord: whether we live therefore, or die, we are the Lord's." (Romans 14:7-8) Meaning that we all belong to God and we bring shame upon him by our actions.

Right with God

People outside the Church need someone right with God. "Having your conversation honest among the Gentiles: that, whereas they speak against you as evildoers, they may by your good works, which they shall behold, glorify God in the day of visitation." (I Peter 2:12) It is amazing that when someone gets into trouble, they seek a Christian for spiritual guidance. Could that Christian be you?

Your family needs an anchor for their assurance of their right relationship to God. Jesus said himself that, "A prophet is not without honor, save in his own country, and in his own house." (Matthew 13:57) In other words, your family knows you well and knows your actions better than anyone else. Why should they take God seriously if you don't? "But take heed lest by any means this liberty of yours become a stumblingblock to them that are weak." (I Corinthians 8:9)

One may ask, "Am I my brother's keeper?" as Cain did after his sin of murdering his brother, Abel. Does God measure us by our love for others? The book of I John 3:17 tells us directly, "But whoso hath this world's good, and seeth his brother have need, and shutteth up his bowels of compassion from him, how dwelleth the love of God in him?" This, too, is listening to the flesh, not the Spirit. A deeper commitment is what is needed, not a superficial gesture, but a sacrificial giving of yourself. The Spirit will overcome the flesh when you find this perfect love. "Herein is our love made perfect, that we may have boldness in the day of judgment: because as he is, so are we in this world." (I John 4:17)

Attitude of Actions

When our attitude is right with God, right actions are to follow. You will see joy and enthusiasm increase as you serve God. This is the spiritual high road God wants you to stay on. Thus, we are focusing on spiritual things, and the lust of the flesh goes by the wayside. It is a true saying about our service to God when, "you are so preoccupied in staying out of sin that you never experience your true service and purpose for the Lord."

If you want to show others that you are not right with God, not thinking spiritually, not on the high road, just show them a poor attitude. I am saying this that you might give God a chance to work in your life, to lift you up, open your spiritual eyes, and keep you on that high road of life. "But Godliness with contentment is great gain." (I Timothy 6:6)

God at Work

Consider the many ways you can observe God working:

1. Hands for Charity – Deuteronomy 15:7-8, "If there be among you a poor man… thou shalt not harden thine heart, nor shut thine hand... Thou shalt open thine hand wide unto him, and shalt surely lend him sufficient for his need." <u>God's love.</u>

2. Eyes to see his power – II Kings 6:16-17, (Syrian army attack) "Fear not: for they that be with us are more than they that be with them. And Elisha prayed, and said, Lord, I pray thee, open his eyes, that he may see." <u>Spiritual power is real.</u>

3. Ears to hear him – Proverbs 15:31, "The ear that heareth the reproof of life abideth among the wise." <u>The wise listen.</u>

4. Lips for your testimony – Psalm 107:2, "Let the redeemed of the Lord say so, whom he hath redeemed from the hand of the enemy." <u>Christians rejoice.</u>

5. Make a stand for prayer – Daniel 6:10, "Now when Daniel knew that the writing was signed, he went into his house; and his windows being open… Kneeled upon his knees three times a day, and prayed…" <u>Godly courage.</u>

6. Be receptive to God's message – I Peter 2:2, "As newborn babes, desire the sincere milk of the word, that ye may grow thereby." <u>Spiritual growth.</u>

7. Desire good works – I Corinthians 3:9, "For we are labourers together with God: ye are God's husbandry, ye are God's building." <u>God is working with others, He wants you to walk with him also.</u>

Judged

The Christian life is open to the public for everyone to see, and you will give a message either positive or negative. God sees even more of your works. Are they spiritual or of the fleshly motives designed for self-exaltation.

The judge will one day try by fire what sort these works are. "Every man's work shall be made manifest: for the day shall declare it, because it shall be revealed by fire; and the fire shall try every man's work of what sort it is." (I Cor. 3:13) This should not be a warning of condemnation, but a directive to be concise about our motives.

God's Divine Ways

"For as the heavens are higher than the earth, so are my ways higher than your ways, and my thoughts than your thoughts." (Isaiah 55:9)

Man is born in this world with natural thoughts and learns the world's ways and philosophies to the point of being indoctrinated. God's thoughts are not considered a part of his life until salvation. Then the Holy Spirit will show the new believer how to grow, but the flesh struggles. "For what man knoweth the things of a man, save the spirit of man which is in him? even so the things of God knoweth no man, but the Spirit of God." (I Cor. 2:11)

The Spirit of God reveals God's thoughts, and this is called Spiritual discernment.

I Corinthians 2:12 tells us; "Now we have received, not the spirit of the world, but the spirit which is of God; that we might know the things that are freely given to us of God." (see also v15 and 16)

The unsaved have only man's natural thoughts. I Corinthians 2:14 tells us, "But the natural man receiveth not the things of the Spirit of God: for they are foolishness unto him: neither can he know them, because they are spiritually discerned."

The Search for Fulfillment

The search for happiness in this world seems to be the main thrust for most people, saved or unsaved. The world's philosophy is; "Eat, drink, and be merry, for tomorrow we die." The desires of the flesh know no limit. Satisfaction is the ultimate goal. But how many people really reach the pinnacle of happiness? The flesh is insatiable and never stops striving for more because it will never be satisfied.

Solomon is probably the best example in the Bible because of his mass experiences. Nothing was restrained from him. "And whatsoever mine eyes desired I kept not from them, I withheld not my heart from any joy; for my heart rejoiced in all my labor: and this was my portion of all my labour." (Eccl. 2:10) So if you have it all, you can be happy, right? If you are rich, you will be happy? After all, these are the fruits of your labor and you are entitled to do as you please, what more is there?

Notice the thoughts of Solomon after he experienced all there was that this world has to offer. "Then I looked on all the works that my hands had wrought, and on the labour that I had laboured to do: and, behold, all was vanity and vexation of spirit, and there was no profit under the sun." (Eccl. 2:11) Unsettling like the wind blowing away.

What is excellent

As God lives is permanent;

Hearts are dust, heart's loves remain;

Heart's love will meet thee again.

Revere the Maker; fetch thine eye

Up to his style, and manner of the sky.

R.W. Emerson

When you seek pleasure to fulfill your desire of the flesh, the satisfaction is dead. You can become immune to stimulation. How many drinks and kinds of drugs do you have to take to find satisfaction? When does overeating stop? Like the man that ate until he could not get out of bed. When he died, they had to tear the walls down to get him out of his bedroom. "And be not drunk with wine, wherein is excess; but be filled with the Spirit." (Eph. 5:18)

God Shall Provide

The Bible tells us in Ecclesiastes 5:18-20, "Behold that which I have seen: it is good and comely for one to eat and to drink, and to enjoy the good of all his labour that he taketh under the sun all the days of his life, which God giveth him: for it is his portion. Every man also to whom God hath given riches and wealth, and hath given him power to eat thereof, and to take his portion, and to rejoice in his labour; this is the gift of God. For he shall not much remember the days of his life; because God answereth him in the joy of his heart." "Wherefore be ye not unwise, but understanding what the will of the Lord is." (Eph. 5:17)

Rich Toward God

Some will approach life to get fame and fortune. It is not a sin to have wealth, but it is a travesty in the eyes of the Lord to focus entirely on self-pride and arrogance. For example, the rich man who needed bigger barns to hold all his goods; "And he thought within himself, saying, What shall I do, because I have no room where to bestow my fruits? And he said, This will I do: I will pull down my barns, and build greater; and there will I bestow all my fruits and my goods. And I will say to my soul, Soul, thou hast much goods laid up for many years; take thine ease, eat, drink, and be merry. But God said unto him, Thou fool, this night shall thy soul be required of thee: then whose shall those things be, which thou hast provided? So is he that layeth up treasure for himself, and is not rich toward God." (Luke 12:17-21)

Solomon's Temple had gold in the mortar, lavish wealth, but was destroyed in 587 B.C. by Nebuchadnezzar II. Solomon had servants for every wish, 700 wives and 300 concubines, 40,000 horses and chariots, 12,000 horsemen, etc. He took a good look at his life and concluded that it was all vanity and vexation (meaning feed upon or grasp after), of the spirit. In other words, these actions can work on your soul and integrate your very spirit to the point of being consumed and will change your attitude before God. "There is that maketh himself rich, yet hath nothing: there is that maketh himself poor, yet hath great riches. The ransom of a man's life are his riches: but the poor heareth not rebuke. (Prov. 13:7-8)

Futility in Life

What's the difference between a 92 year old man praying to God to "go ahead and take me, I have lived my life well and am ready to die;" than a 42 year old man that says, "God take my life, I am ready to go, I can't take it anymore"?

Our life separated to God, or our life separated from God, makes all the difference. When you are the potter, your design may be an inferior attempt at life, but if you let God be the potter and architect, he will carefully cover the details to a sculptured life unto honor.

Consider the signs of a life apart from being God's workmanship: The futile experience of man; "Because I have called, and ye refused; I have stretched out my hand, and no man regarded." (Prov. 1:24)

1. Life is utterly futile – what's the use in trying

2. Repetitive – same old thing every day

3. Sorrowful – no happiness, no joy, no good

4. Grievous and frustrating – getting nowhere

5. Uncertain – no peace at all on anything

6. Without purpose – what's the use

7. Incurable – basket case, depression

8. Unjust – will cheat to get ahead

9. Mere existence – surviving day to day, not living God's plan is the higher road that man can find for himself through Jesus Christ; "For we are his workmanship, created in Christ Jesus unto good works, which God hath before ordained that we should walk in them." (Eph. 2:10)

Plants have one sense – a sense of existence

Animals have two senses -- existence and self-awareness

Mankind has three senses – existence, self-awareness, and God-awareness

"Behold the fowls of the air: for they sow not, neither do they reap, nor gather into barns; yet your heavenly Father feedeth them. Are ye not much better than they?" (Mat.6:26)

Take the High Road
Doing the Right Thing

Chapter Two
Trying to do the Right Thing Goes Nowhere Without God.

Taking Matters into Your Own Hands

Have you ever tried to do the right thing by helping someone out and it seems to backfire? A popular saying, "good guys finish last," holds a lot of truth.

In Exodus 2:11-15, we find Moses trying to identify himself as the one who reckons with evil by committing sin himself. "And it came to pass in those days, when Moses was grown, that he went out unto his brethren, and looked on their burdens: and he spied an Egyptian smiting an Hebrew, one of his brethren. And he looked this way and that way, and when he saw that there was no man, he slew the Egyptian, and hid him in the sand. And when he went out the second day, behold, two men of the Hebrews strove together: and he said to him that did the wrong, Wherefore smitest thou thy fellow? And he said, Who made thee a prince and a judge over us?

intendest thou to kill me, as thou killedst the Egyptian? And Moses feared, and said, Surely this thing is known. Now when Pharaoh heard this thing, he sought to slay Moses. But Moses fled from the face of Pharaoh, and dwelt in the land of Midian: and he sat down by a well."

Character Rises Above

Being said, our actions are accountable to God, and they are also accountable to man. Moses has now made a life-changing action that will mandate his future. One could ask at this point about Moses' character; he couldn't stand by and watch one of his brethren being mistreated. His character was given to him by God and that is the most defining reason why God called him to service. God saw in him a great faith motivated by his character. "By faith Moses, when he was come to years, refused to be called the son of Pharaoh's daughter; Choosing rather to suffer affliction with the people of God, than to enjoy the pleasures of sin for a season; Esteeming the reproach of Christ greater riches than the treasures in Egypt: for he had respect unto the recompense of the reward." (Heb. 11:24-26)

God's Mercy

It may be hard to understand, but God had a plan in all of this. "So then it is not of him that willeth, nor of him that runneth, but of God that sheweth mercy. For the scripture saith unto Pharaoh, Even for this same purpose have I raised thee up, that I might shew my power in thee, and that my name might be declared throughout all the earth." (Rom. 9:16-17) Did God care for the Israelites and want to rescue them very similarly to what Moses did? Four hundred years of slavery and he had not left them without hope. The deliverer has arrived, but only on God's terms, with God's man, in God's timing. "And his mercy is on them that fear him from generation to generation." (Luke 1:50)

The high road is not easy to take; it may cause you to separate from others while trying to do the right thing by man and especially by God.

"Do right regardless of the consequences. Do right if the stars fall." 1 (Bob Jones)

You can't follow the world side-stepping God's intentions for your life. The world is who got you in trouble to start with. Turn away because God is right, he is just, he is loving, he cares, he is merciful, and he forgives. If we all get what we deserve, we would be in trouble, but we have received his mercy.

Out of Control

What do you do when things get out of control? How did this happen? I was trying to do the right thing, and besides I thought nobody knew my secret sin. "And he looked this way and that way, and when he saw that there was no man, he slew the Egyptian, and hid him in the sand." (Ex. 2:12) "…and be sure your sin will find you out." (Num. 32:23)

---

[1] "Do Right," The Sword of the Lord Publishers, Murfreesboro TN, 1971, pg. 10

One day you can decide that you will turn over a new leaf and start living a morally clean life and start praying more, just to find out that the closer to God you want to become, the more sin is exposed by the Holy Spirit. "The closer to the light, more dirt shows up," is a very true statement. Give up old habits, old ways, change friends, read self-help books, to plan my success to follow God. James chapter 4:13-17, should put a Christian back on track when the self-pride and self-independence go too far. "Go to now, ye that say, To day or to morrow we will go into such a city, and continue there a year, and buy and sell, and get gain: Whereas ye know not what shall be on the morrow. For what is your life? It is even a vapour, that appeareth for a little time, and then vanisheth away. For that ye ought to say, If the Lord will, we shall live, and do this, or that. But now ye rejoice in your boastings: all such rejoicing is evil. Therefore to him that knoweth to do good, and doeth it not, to him it is sin."

How many times in life have we decided that my way is better than God's way and I pray he will bless my decisions to do my own thing, when all the while, deep in your soul, you know the Holy Spirit is telling you to yield and listen to God? The result is out of control, because you have entertained your road way too long and things have gone too far now. It is never too late to pull the plug on your plan, yield to God, and ask for guidance. Then wait until he answers.

Grace Abounds

It is a good thing that God knows the believer enough to see all the sins that so easily beset him/her. God's grace can move into all areas that have led us captive. Ephesians 4:7-10 addresses the power of God through Christ for us. "But unto every one of us is given grace according to the measure of the gift of Christ. Wherefore he saith, When he ascended up on high, he led captivity captive, and gave gifts unto men. (Now that he ascended, what is it but that he also descended first into the lower parts of the earth? He that descended is the same also that ascended up far above all heavens, that he might fill all things.)" Simply saying, he has omnipotence over death and life, omniscience over all the earth, omnipresence in your life; he has captured what has captured you. Victory belongs to Jesus, and that includes the believer if the yielding is present.

"And the Lord said, I have surely seen the affliction of my people which are in Egypt, and have heard their cry by reason of their taskmasters; for I know their sorrows; And I am come down to deliver them out of the hand of the Egyptians, and to bring them up out of that land unto a good land and a large, unto a land flowing with milk and honey…" (Ex. 3:7-8) Grace will bring peace when we direct our lives toward God. Change is there when God takes over. When God started on Moses, forty years had passed before he saw a vessel usable for a divine purpose. How long does it take to humble your heart to God? The patience is on his side, growing is his intention for you.

1. Suppression leads to - stagnation, no life flow

2. Yielding leads to – right living, right decisions, success in life

Romans 8:28 is true; "And we know that all things work together for good to them that love God, to them who are the called according to his purpose."

My Way or God's

I want it my way or I will not do it at all, seems to be the main stand today. Free speech, free sexuality, free religion, etc. describes the sensuality of human souls today. This independent, defiant behavior didn't just start; the first born child of Adam and Eve was a free thinker full of pride to the point of murder.

"And Adam knew Eve his wife; and she conceived, and bare Cain, and said, I have gotten a man from the Lord. And she again bare his brother Abel. And Abel was a keeper of sheep, but Cain was a tiller of the ground. And in process of time it came to pass, that Cain brought of the fruit of the ground an offering unto the Lord. And Abel, he also brought of the firstlings of his flock and of the fat thereof. And the Lord had respect unto Abel and to his offering: but unto Cain and to his offering he had not respect. And Cain was very wroth, and his countenance fell. And the Lord said unto Cain, Why art thou wroth? and why is thy countenance fallen? If thou doest well, shalt thou not be accepted? and if thou doest not well, sin lieth at the door. And unto thee shall be his desire, and thou shalt rule over him. And Cain talked with Abel his brother: and it came to pass, when they were in the field, that Cain rose up against Abel his brother, and slew him." (Ge. 4:1-8)

Who is the authority after all? Shouldn't the Christian separate "unto" God, or separate "from" God? To put it directly, it is God's way or sin will have its way with you according to verse 7. I will give you the offering that I want to give whether God likes it or not. My brother may be acceptable unto God, but by God's grace, I should be acceptable too!

The Lord gave Cain a second chance to get it right and didn't threaten to take his life, but warned him of his wrong sinful choice. Think on this verse in Luke 12:5, "But I will forewarn you whom ye shall fear: Fear him, which after he hath killed hath power to cast into hell; yea, I say unto you, Fear him."

Judge Me Not

People today do not accept that there is a judge that will make them accountable for their sin, and their very souls will be in the balance of heaven and hell. "It is appointed unto men once to die, but after this the judgment." (Heb. 9:27) What kind of life does someone live that has the weight of sin upon them; with guilt, shame, pride, etc.? That is no more than a futile existence. The animal thinks on surviving, the little ant is wise: "There be four things which are little upon the earth, but they are exceeding wise." (Prov.30:24) Referring to the ants, conies (rabbits), locusts, and spiders which can foresee their future.

So is it a matter of not foreseeing or refusing to see and accept? It is a true example of a person driving their car right into the ditch, like many people have done with their life because of poor and unwise decisions.

Ever Growing Sin Problem

It comes back to God's high road or man's ever-diverting low road that leads to dangerous risks, constant struggle, dodging trouble continuously, and no peace. The threat of sin that "lieth at the door," is like a leopard ready to pounce at any given moment that you sin. When one opens the door to sin, then what have you done?

In the south, a plant called "kudzu," of Asian origin, was introduced in the late 1800's to help soil erosion. Some 85 million seedlings were eventually passed out. The dust bowl was an era of desperate need of something to help. By 1946, 3 million acres had been planted. Someone made the decision to do the obvious to help, but this plant is totally invasive, completely engulfing whole trees and anything that gets in its way. Corrupting and killing as it spreads; the plant was considered in 1970 as a noxious weed, a dangerous vine indeed.

Separate Unto God

The wisdom of God knows that Christians can get caught up into a world full of temptations, false promises, and wrong choices. We can find ourselves entangled to the point that only God can separate and cultivate to help us see a clear path once again. "But every man is tempted, when he is drawn away of his own lust, and enticed. Then when lust hath conceived, it bringeth forth sin: and sin, when it is finished, bringeth forth death. Do not err, my beloved brethren. (Jam. 1:14-15)

The Bible explains in I John 2:15-17, "Love not the world, neither the things that are in the world. If any man love the world, the love of the Father is not in him. For all that is in the world, the lust of the flesh, and the lust of the eyes, and the pride of life, is not of the Father, but is of the world. And the world passeth away, and the lust thereof: but he that doeth the will of God abideth for ever."

There is no way the unbeliever can ever break free this torrent of ever-present bondage on his own. Start by:

I. <u>Accepting Christ as Savior</u> – "Therefore if any man be in Christ, he is a new creature: old things are passed away; behold, all things are become new." (II Corinthians 5:17)

II. <u>Letting God Start Working</u> – "Submit yourselves therefore to God. Resist the devil, and he will flee from you." (James 4:7)

III. <u>Mortifying the Flesh</u> – "Knowing this, that our old man is crucified with him, that the body of sin might be destroyed, that henceforth we should not serve sin." (Romans 6:6)

IV. <u>Reading the Word of God</u> – "Thy word is a lamp unto my feet, and a light unto my path." (Psalms 119:105)

V. <u>Gain Knowledge and Wisdom</u> – "The fear of the Lord is the beginning of knowledge: but fools despise wisdom and instruction." (Proverbs 1:7)

VI. <u>Joining a Bible Believing Church</u> – "Not forsaking the assembling of ourselves together, as the manner of some is; but exhorting one another: and so much the more, as ye see the day approaching." (Hebrews 10:25)

VII. <u>Yielding to the Holy Spirit</u> – "I beseech you therefore, brethren, by the mercies of God, that ye present your bodies a living sacrifice, holy, acceptable unto God, which is your reasonable service. And be not conformed to this world: but be ye transformed by the renewing of your mind, that ye may prove what is that good, and acceptable, and perfect, will of God." (Romans 12:1-2)

Take the High Road
Doing the Right Thing

Chapter Three
You are Considered Valuable to Heaven

Misunderstood

Earthly things of value are easy to see, but there is too much emphasis on such temporal objects. It is funny how you come into this world all helpless with nothing, and you go out of this world without any earthly treasures because you can't take it with you. Or, can you take something with you that only God and those around that have a discerning eye can see?

The Bible tells us in John chapter one, of Jesus, the Word, the Son of God, who brought light into this sin darkened world. "And the light shineth in darkness; and the darkness comprehended not." (John 1:5) The world watched Jesus, but was truly blind to who he really was.

But, there is an individual who seems to go unnoticed too much. Where there are volumes on Jesus, how much attention is put on this man John? "There was a man sent from God, whose name was John. The same came for a witness, to bear witness of the Light, that all men through him might believe. He was not that Light, but was sent to bear witness of that Light." (John 1:6-8)

Once a person is saved, born again, he/she has entered into a spiritual realm that is opposite of this world. The world does not understand where you are coming from when you start following Christ, when you start glorifying the Son of God as John did. Your deep priorities have changed and your cares of this world have shifted from temporal thinking to eternal thoughts.

Why couldn't Jesus survive here? Why does the world see the spirituality as a threat? It's okay to be religious and follow some kind of rituals or wear strange attire, but to mention the name Jesus, you would think you had personally offended the person.

Picture a big, tall, darkened forest with one medium-sized white tree standing strong and brave. This tree is obviously different, more beautiful, more valuable, than all the rest. The tendency of this world is to cut it down because it interrupts the continuity of the natural flow of the forest. The Christian has more beauty inside and out because he is in the care of God himself. When Jesus spoke of the lilies of the field, he said; "And why take ye thought for raiment? Consider the lilies of the field, how they grow; they toil not, neither do they spin: And yet I say unto you, That even Solomon in all his glory was not arrayed like one of these." (Mat. 6:28-29)

Called Out

The Christian has been anointed to live here as a witness of the truth. That can't be denied by the world. Jesus said in John seventeen of the sanctification; "I have given them thy word; and the world hath hated them, because they are not of the world, even as I am not of the world. I pray not that thou shouldest take them out of the world, but that thou shouldest keep them from the evil. They are not of the world, even as I am not of the world. Sanctify them through thy truth: thy word is truth. As thou hast sent me into the world, even so have I also sent them into the world." (John 17:14-18)

John the Baptist dared to live as a witness, a forerunner of Jesus Christ, separate from the sins of the people, but offering them a message of repentance. "His manner reminded everyone of the earlier prophets, and stirred the population deeply. Most startling, however, was his announcement that God's message was about to come, and the hour of judgment was upon the people. Another was to follow him, John announced, that would bring in the new era." 2 (William P. Barker)

Who's in Control

To the Christian, the corruption of the world is not desirable. How easy the habits and sins were before you were saved, before the Holy Spirit came to live inside

---

2 *Everyone in the Bible*, William P. Barker, Fleming H. Revell Co. Westwood, NJ, pg. 194

of you. But, now you can see and feel as if you were walking in a landfill with all the offensive vices of the world reeking at your being, wanting to turn away for self-preservation. Yet, somehow, you might have some baggage from your pre-spiritual life hanging on your life that you can't come to grips with. But, the Holy Spirit knows it's there and keeps reminding you to address such.

The question is, do you control your life? Your repentance included what? Just the things that you thought were distasteful, and then decided to keep back things that you could not depart with? After all, I am only human and God will understand.

"Let not sin therefore reign in your mortal body, that ye should obey it in the lusts thereof." (Rom. 6:12) This verse is truly pointing out that you will obey sin because there are lusts that are attached. Temptation is the test. If you are tempted to sin, lust has taken you there, and lust leads to sin. "But every man is tempted, when he is drawn away of his own lust, and enticed. Then when lust hath conceived, it bringeth forth sin: and sin, when it is finished, bringeth forth death." (Jam. 1:14-15)

Why does a person have to clean up their life just because he accepts Christ? It is amazing that we are not doing the cleaning, but we are allowing God to do it. The common lump of coal has turned into a diamond in the rough. The Master is trying to mold and shape us by trimming off the areas that keep us unholy, perfect, and sanctified. He goes from hammer and chisel, to eventually, sandpaper and polish. "But the Comforter, which is the Holy Ghost, whom the Father will send in my name, he shall teach you all things, and bring all things to your remembrance, whatsoever I have said unto you." (John 14:26)

How valuable are you to the world? This depends on how much money they can make off of you and how you can commit to their agenda. This is how it works:

1. Starts with an ungodly agenda – politics, theater, music, art, (II Tim. 2:4)

2. Fueled by Satan's ambitions – his plan must progress, time is short, (Rev. 12:12)

3. Humans are disposable – war, talent, worth, etc. Tower of Babel, (Gen. 11)

4. Ever-evolving cycle – keep up or get left behind as non- valuable, John 16:33 – "...In the world ye shall have tribulation: but be of good cheer; I have overcome the world."

Make no mistake about it, we belong to God, but a Christian can be lured away by the worldly lusts. Consider where you stand in this world, between earth and heaven, tried by both God and the devil.

- "But ye have an unction from the Holy One, and ye know all things. I have not written unto you because ye know not the truth, but because ye know it, and that no lie is of the truth. Who is a

liar but he that denieth that Jesus is the Christ? He is antichrist, that denieth the Father and the Son." I John 2:20-22
- "We know that whosoever is born of God sinneth not; but he that is begotten of God keepeth himself, and that wicked one toucheth him not. And we know that we are of God, and the whole world lieth in wickedness."
I John 5:18-19
- "Either make the tree good, and his fruit good; or else make the tree corrupt, and his fruit corrupt: for the tree is known by his fruit." Matthew 12:33

One would try to argue the fact, that the unbelieving world has a lot of good in it, and he would be correct, but it is the power of the Holy Spirit holding back evil or else total chaos would be taking place. "For the mystery of iniquity doth already work: only he who now letteth <u>will let</u>, until he be taken out of the way." (II Thess. 2:7) This will end at the day of rapture when God will reveal the Wicked one. "And then shall that Wicked be revealed, whom the Lord shall consume with the spirit of his mouth, and shall destroy with the brightness of his coming."
(II Thess. 2:8)

Light Shines in a Darkened Place

"Let your light so shine before men, that they may see your good works, and glorify your Father which is heaven." (Mat. 5:16) Jesus starts off to say that you are the light of the world. Your light came by accepting Christ as he placed within you the ever-glorifying Holy Spirit, that has changed you and gave a new hope and purpose to live.

It is a tragedy that the light is barely seen in some that are being oppressed or misguided by circumstances. The book of Isaiah chapter six starts out with this verse, "In the year that King Uzziah died I saw also the Lord sitting upon a throne, high and lifted up, and his train filled the temple." (Isa. 6:1) Isaiah had a clear vision of the Lord sitting upon the throne with angels surrounding him crying, "Holy, holy, holy" is the Lord of hosts: the whole earth is full of his glory." (Isa. 6:3)

Two questions arise after this incident and vision:
1. Why didn't Isaiah see all this before? - Could it be that he focused his attention on the light of the wrong king? (earthly)
2. Was the whole earth full of the glory of God always or just when Isaiah had the vision? – The glory has always been here as it is today, but man can't see this accumulative light from God shining over the whole earth because of the darkness of man's heart.

The response from Isaiah is most astounding; "Then said I, Woe is me! for I am undone; because I am a man of unclean lips, and I dwell in the midst of a people of unclean lips: for mine eyes have seen the King, the Lord of hosts. Then flew one of the seraphims unto me, having a live coal in his hand, which he had taken with the tongs from off the altar: And he laid it upon my mouth, and said, Lo, this hath touched thy lips; and thine iniquity is taken away, and thy sin purged." (Isa. 6:5-7)

What holds a person back from glorifying God? Isaiah saw the glory, which was a life-changing experience to serve. God had a plan to use Isaiah. He saw him as a most valuable asset in an effort to bring Israel to repentance. "Also I heard the voice of the Lord, saying, Whom shall I send, and who will go for us? Then said I, Here am I; send me. And he said, Go, and tell this people, Hear ye indeed, but understand not; and see ye indeed, but perceive not. Make the heart of this people fat, and make their ears heavy, and shut their eyes; lest they see with their eyes, and hear with their ears, and understand with their heart, and convert, and be healed." (Isa. 6:8-10)

The glimpse of glory for Isaiah showed that God cared for Isaiah to open his eyes and that he cared for Israel and wanted them to open their heart and be healed. We all are valuable to heaven, but we have to meet God on his spiritual terms. "Humble yourselves in the sight of the Lord, and he shall lift you up." (Jam. 4:10)

God's Ultimate Care

John 1:5, "And the light shineth in darkness; and the darkness comprehended it not."

God cares so much for his people that he sent his only begotten Son into a world that did not understand him, wouldn't receive him, and finally put him to death. He knew this would be the reaction to this glorious gift of His Son, so he went to the ultimate extent for mankind by raising Jesus Christ from the dead as a living Savior. All man has to do is open their heart, accept his word, and be Saved. "But the righteousness which is of faith speaketh on this wise, Say not in thine heart, Who shall ascend into heaven? (that is, to bring Christ down from above:) Or, who shall descend into the deep? (that is, to bring up Christ again from the dead.) But what saith it? The word is nigh thee, even in thy mouth, and in thy heart: that is, the word of faith, which we preach; that if thou shalt confess with thy mouth the Lord Jesus, and shalt believe in thine heart that God hath raised him from the dead, thou shalt be saved." (Rom. 10:6-9)

Take the High Road
Doing the Right Thing

Chapter Four
Intentions

Good Intentions

The whole world has promised someone at some time something, but has broken the promise. Good intentions mean well, but in reality, don't last long and don't mean that much to God. Jesus made a point of this in Luke 9:59-62, "And he said unto another, Follow me. But he said, Lord, suffer me first to go and bury my father. Jesus said unto him, Let the dead bury their dead: but go thou and preach the kingdom of God. And another also said, Lord, I will follow thee; but let me first go bid them farewell, which are at home at my house. And Jesus said unto him, No man, having put his hand to the plough, and looking back, is fit for the kingdom of God."

To many, this statement from Jesus seems harsh, but Jesus knows:

1. If you have to delay the decision to follow the Lord, there will be no commitment.

2. You are giving the enemy a chance to alter your situation and you will doubt and be unsettled to serve God.

3. There will be no determination to follow through, and experience all that God wants to do to transform your life. (Rom. 12:2)

Allow God to plough and reveal his intentions as the Apostle Paul speaks of in Philippians 3:13-14, "Brethren, I count not myself to have apprehended: <u>but this one thing I do</u>, forgetting those things which are behind, and reaching forth unto those things which are before. I press toward the mark for the prize of the high calling of God in Christ Jesus." What we see with Paul, is a determination to push forward, plan ahead, and let the Holy Spirit lead.

One Thing at a Time

A farmer has to plow one row at a time to plant his field. God's plan is not something we can obtain all at once, but the servant knows the whole plan has to be fulfilled as the farmer knows that the whole field needs planted and harvested. What the farmer does not know is if there will be storms, drought, etc.; but this does not keep him from his intended plan.

"I will serve God someday," is not a plan. A good idea, a faith that is distracted, an intention most honorable, but of no affect. "Even so faith, if it hath not works, is dead, being alone. Yea, a man may say, Thou hast faith, and I have works: shew me thy faith without thy works, and I will shew thee my faith by my works.

Thou believest that there is one God; thou doest well: the devils also believe, and tremble." (Jam. 2:17-19)
"And the point is that we will never realize how truly committed we are to Him until we are tested, until we are tried in the crucible of pressure and stress. God tests us in order that we might find out our level of commitment – and hopefully move forward and onward and deeper from there." 3 (Charles Stanley)

Today Has Come

We all have been at a funeral of a loved one and remarked, "I wish I had spent more time with that person; now it's too late." Life gets in the way, busy days absorb time, and before you know it, the future has become the past. All is not lost, because the Lord is ever-patient. "God never hurries. There are no deadlines against that he must work. Only to know this is to quiet our spirits and relax our nerves." -- A.W. Tozer

Everyone knows their own life well and can look back at all our experiences, jobs, family, hardships, and achievements. One thing you don't know is what God can do with your life as a surrendered human being. Let Jesus say it in his own words; "And he said to them all, If any man will come after me, let him deny himself, and take up his cross daily, and follow me. For whosoever will save his life shall lose it: but whosoever will lose his life for my sake, the same shall save it."

3 Charles F, Stanley, *Confronting Casual Christianity*, Broadman Press, 1985, pg. 120

(Luke 9:23-24)

What is that other life that Jesus is referring to in these verses? Could it be that some decisions could have been made differently? Or if you could have seen where God wanted you to step out in faith and trust the outcome to him? The high road is not the road usually traveled by people, because we walk by sight and not by faith. II Corinthians 5:7 tells us the opposite, to "walk by faith, not by sight." Remember that it is never too late to follow the Lord. To do the right thing will be a challenge, but it is worth it.

The definition of insanity is: To do the same thing this year as you did last year and expect a better outcome. As the old cowboy said, "When the old horse is dead, it is time to dismount."

"Let the dead bury their dead: but go thou and preach the kingdom of God." (Luke 9:60)

"O, brethren, be great believers! Little faith will bring your soul to heaven, but great faith will bring heaven to your soul." C.H. Spurgeon

Use It or Lose It

You can take two people with similar backgrounds and lifestyles and sit them in the same church, listening to the same sermon at the same time, and one will be moved and inspired and the other person is looking at his watch wondering when the service will be over. Is this a mystery, or could it be that one came to church intending to let God speak to him and the other one heard the word and was distracted about personal intentions and plans? Jesus addresses our heart's condition in a parable with unmistakable truth. "A sower went out to sow his seed: and as he sowed, some fell by the wayside; and it was trodden down, and the fowls of the air devoured it. And some fell upon a rock; and as soon as it was sprung up, it withered away, because it lacked moisture. And some fell among thorns; and the thorns sprang up with it, and choked it. And other fell on good ground, and sprang up, and bare fruit an hundredfold. And when he had said these things, he cried, He that hath ears to hear, let him hear." (Luke 8:5-8)

How fast can money disappear from your hand? Seems like any plan to invest or save can be taken away by one unforeseen breakdown or repair in one moment. Some people will go to church, listen to the word preached, and only receive enough inspiration for a weekly fix, and not enough inspiration to change their life.

"Well, that preacher doesn't relay the word right," or, "well, the service had too many people praising and not meaning it." Or any other way to blame others for your self-made view of what is right. Jesus said in Matthew 5:6, "Blessed are they which do hunger and thirst after righteousness: for they shall be filled." Be honest with yourself. Do you want the Lord to help you? Do you want to understand wisdom and truth that only comes from on high? Notice Jesus' explanation to the sower parable in one verse; "But that on the good ground are they, which in an honest and good heart, having heard the word, keep it, and bring forth fruit with patience." (Luke 8:15)

Your New Walk

There are many people that have experienced true conversion, and the change in their life is obvious and evident. Some toy with the spiritual facts, but never accept, and there is no change. "No man, when he hath lighted a candle, covereth it with a vessel, or putteth it under a bed; but setteth it on a candlestick, that they which enter in may see the light. For nothing is secret, that shall not be made manifest; neither any thing hid, that shall not be known and come abroad. Take heed therefore how you hear: for whosoever hath, to him shall be given; and whosoever hath not, from him shall be taken even that which he seemeth to have." (Luke 8:16-18) A serious commitment will have to be made at some point with all the support and guidance of the Holy Spirit, encouraging and giving strength as you journey in life.

"This I say then, Walk in the Spirit, and ye shall not fulfil the lust of the flesh. For the flesh lusteth against the Spirit, and the Spirit against the flesh: and these are contrary the one to the other: so that ye cannot do the things that ye would." (Gal. 5:16-17) You have good intentions, but then the scripture here says that a person once saved, is facing a battle with himself.

The challenge:

1. <u>Walk in the Spirit</u> – this is a new spiritual bond with God, a new guidance by the Holy Spirit. (Paraclete)

2. Ye shall not fulfill the lust of the flesh – the unity with the Spirit, (Eph. 4:3), needs to stay intact, your best is required to mortify the flesh.

3. You have walked in the flesh all your life so far – Now there are boundaries to think about; you will gain wisdom as you walk. (Phil. 4:8)

Take the High Road
Doing the Right Thing

Chapter Five

When the Devil is Camped Outside Your Door

The most amazing feeling in this life is when you are walking with God and everything seems to be a mountain top experience. Success is a reality, your health is good, family and friends are happy, money is steady and secure, and out of nowhere someone comes to challenge you and your belief and well-being. We all live with negative people, but when they become your enemy and try to destroy you, things have to be turned over to God only for refuge.

II Chronicles 31:20-21 records the lifestyle and success of Hezekiah. "And thus did Hezekiah throughout all Judah, and wrought that which was good and right and truth before the Lord his God. And in every work that he began in the service of the house of God, and in the law, and in the commandments, to seek his God, he did it with all his heart, and prospered." Life couldn't be better. God was honored by all of Judah led by an honorable and godly king. Then the enemy showed up.

You look out on the surrounding cities and find an army of 200,000 encamped and planning against you--what is your first instinct? We all have been faced with insurmountable odds at times, and fear seems to be the first emotion that surfaces. Then the acknowledgement that something has to be done. Ignoring the facts doesn't make it go away.

Sennacherib came and proposed to fight against Jerusalem, according to II Chronicles 32, but Hezekiah had a plan; "He took counsel with his princes and his mighty men to stop the waters of the fountains which were without the city: and they did help him. So there was gathered much people together, who stopped all the fountains, and the brook that ran through the midst of the land, saying, Why should the kings of Assyria come, and find much water?" (II Chron. 32:3-4)

True wisdom is living your life under God's protection, being dedicated to his almighty power and truth, but all the while knowing that the enemy lurks outside and seeks weakness. "Be sober, be vigilant; because your adversary the devil, as a roaring lion, walketh about, seeking whom he may devour: Whom resist steadfast in the faith, knowing that the same afflictions are accomplished in your brethren that are in the world." (I Peter 5:8-9)

Awareness

The devil will always be against God and test his boundaries, and if you stand for the Lord and his ways, he will test you, too. Ignoring the enemy doesn't make him go away, it just leaves you defenseless.

The flash flood warnings were on the television and radio while the man lounged on his recliner paying little attention to the news cast. The dog was pounding at the door and howling, and before he could get out of his chair, he noticed the carpet was wet. He slushed as he stepped to the door and opened it, and in came 2 inches of water and a surfing dog. What happens to the person that knows where their weakness lies, knows the sin that so easily besets them, and chooses to not deal with it? Can you cut off the devil? Hezekiah knew the Assyrians needed water to survive, so he went for the strongest resource that he had with his people agreeing and wisely cooperating.

Taking the high road in your life means not to leave yourself vulnerable in any area. If you keep stepping in that pot hole, for crying out loud, learn to walk around it or fill it in! Whose fault is it when you are caught unaware when the enemy shows up to slow you down and possibly stop your Christian growth? "Draw nigh to God, and he will draw nigh to you. Cleanse your hands, ye sinners; and purify your hearts, ye double minded." (Jam. 4:8)

The Sinful Truth

You might not realize your state in the sight of God, but he has watched the generations of your family for many years. Think on this deep fact: Exodus 20 in the first commandment, "...For I the Lord thy God am a jealous God, visiting the iniquities of the fathers upon the children unto the third and fourth generation of them that hate me; and shewing mercy unto thousands

of them that love me, and keep my commandments." (Ex. 20:5-6)
- ➢ Sin has originated at the Garden of Eden with Adam and Eve.
- ➢ The sin is carried in the blood from the original sin.
- ➢ Your ancestors, at some time, had partaken and entertained sin.
- ➢ Relatives died unsaved, still guilty in their sins.
- ➢ You have tendencies to be vulnerable to certain temptations, some more than others.
- ➢ A growing Christian sees these sins and weaknesses in their body and prays for forgiveness and strength.
- ➢ Mortify the flesh – "Knowing this, that our old man is crucified with him, that the body of sin might be destroyed." (Rom. 6:6)
- ➢ Total abstinence of sin, God will honor. "Blessed is the man that walketh not in the counsel of the ungodly…" (Psa. 1:1-3)
- ➢ The blood of Christ reconciles. (Eph. 2:16)

Politics

Sennacherib, King of Assyria, does not act alone on his quest to conquer Jerusalem. As he sent his servants to Jerusalem, saying unto all Judah; "Thus saith Sennacherib king of Assyria, Whereon do ye trust, that ye abide in the siege in Jerusalem? Doth not Hezekiah persuade you to give over yourselves to die by famine and by thirst, saying, The Lord our God shall deliver us out of the hand of the king of Assyria? (II Chron.

(32:10-11) "Now therefore let not Hezekiah deceive you, nor persuade you on this manner, neither yet believe him: for no god of any nation or kingdom was able to deliver his people out of mine hand, and out of the hand of my fathers: how much less shall your God deliver you out of mine hand? And his servants spake more against the Lord God, and against his servant Hezekiah." (II Chron. 32:15-16)

The enemy has the world convinced that the goal of this life depends upon finance, fame, and fortune. Political power is dictated, but there will always be followers of a better, more efficient society. They seem to overlook morals and spiritual principles. This worldly, devil motivated society has an end whether anyone wants to admit it or accept the truth. "And the world passeth away, and the lust thereof: but he that doeth the will of God abideth for ever."(I John 2:17) The world's influence is difficult to resist. But, the Christian is no longer of this world, speaking in systematic terms. Remember who the guide is that works in you. The Holy Spirit is not of this world.

"For it is God which worketh in you both to will and to do of his good pleasure. Do all things without murmurings and disputings: That ye may be blameless and harmless, the sons of God, without rebuke, in the midst of a crooked and perverse nation, among whom ye shine as lights in the world; Holding forth the word of life; that I may rejoice in the day of Christ, that I have not run in vain, neither labored in vain." (Phil. 2:13-16)

How to Approach the Situation

So the Christian's approach in battle, when the devil is camped at your door, needs to be the same as Hezekiah. Hezekiah the king and Isaiah the prophet prayed and cried to heaven. God had seen and heard all the blasphemy going on down below, and his servants were in danger. "And the Lord sent an angel, which cut off all the mighty men of valour, and the leaders and captains in the camp of the king of Assyria. So he returned with shame of face to his own land. And when he was come into the house of his god, they that came forth of his own bowels slew him there with the sword." (II Chron. 32:21)

Prayer and steadfastness prevail against any enemy that decides to put God to the test.

History has recorded that 185,000 soldiers died on that battle field by a Bubonic plague carried by field mice. Amazing how God can take the smallest object to bring down an overwhelming threat.

"Submit yourselves therefore to God. Resist the devil, and he will flee from you." James 4:7

The Great Lie

The Bible tells us in James 4:17, "Therefore to him that knoweth to do good, and doeth it not, to him it is sin." This would include turning to God in times of doubt and weakness. Some would say that, "I didn't sin on purpose, it just happened." Let's go back to the origination of sin in the book of Genesis. We deal with the devil every day, and what does he want us to believe? Whatever God says he wants us to do, do the opposite or add to God's instruction, which harmonizes it.

"Now the serpent was more subtil than any beast of the field which the Lord God had made. And he said unto the woman, Yea, hath God said, Ye shall not eat of every tree of the garden? And the woman said unto the serpent, We may eat of the fruit of the trees of the garden: but the fruit of the tree which is in the midst of the garden, <u>God hath said, Ye shall not eat of it, neither shall ye touch it, lest ye die.</u> And the serpent said unto the woman, Ye shall not surely die: for God doth know that in the day ye eat thereof, then your eyes shall be opened, and ye shall be as gods, knowing good and evil." (Gen. 3:1-5)

Two things noticeable here:

1. The persuasion to question God – vs. 4, "Ye shall not surely die."

2. The mistranslation of God's word – vs. 3, "...Neither shall ye touch it."

One would conclude that if Eve hadn't misquoted God, would the serpent have seen another way to tempt Eve? What can the enemy present to the Christian that sounds so alluring that one can suddenly know better than God and his word? What have we been told all of our life?

An experiment was performed on a German shepherd dog when he was a pup. A rope was tied on him to a stake next to a fence, he was taught to jump, but the rope was not very long, so he could only jump so far off the ground. He grew, and he was still tied down to the stake by the rope. One day, they took the rope off and commanded him to jump. He was a big dog now and it was a short fence, but he couldn't jump over it. He could only jump as far as he was conditioned all of his life by the length of that rope.

We have been told that the world is over populating, but is this true? A study shows that if you placed everyone in the world in one place, giving each person 2.6 feet each, it would only cover 841 square miles, the size of half the city of Jacksonville, Florida.

Society has convinced everyone that someday we will run out of resources, but is this true? The Bible tells us that it all belongs to God. "The earth is the Lord's, and the fulness thereof; the world, and they that dwell therein." (Psa. 24:1) Can mankind save the planet? It is futile to think that people can make or break God's intentions for the earth. Someone has said that we are just rearranging the chairs on the *Titanic*. Can you believe everything that has been told you all your life? The devil would have people believing that serving God, taking the high road, doing the right thing, is too difficult, so take the easy way out.

Have Faith, Endure

By observing the Christian community in today's world, could you get a clear picture of what faith in God really means? Why have so many diverted from their once dedication and commitment to God? The casual approach to worship and the thoughts of turning God off and on, like a spectator sport, has proven that the enemy has crept in unaware and is trying to spoil the house. The danger is that the ones following the Christian today are being conditioned to sin at will, use God when convenient, but live for all pleasure. If you don't like the task, quit. The going gets tough, get out. Choosing to disbelieve the Bible and practice a little faith is never the road to victory.

In the book of Hebrews, we learn the truth, "Wherefore seeing we also are compassed about with so great a cloud of witnesses, let us lay aside every weight, and the sin which doth so easily beset us, and let us run with patience the race that is set before us, Looking unto Jesus the author and finisher of our faith; who for the joy that was set before him endured the cross, despising the shame, and is set down at the right hand of the throne of God. <u>For consider him that endured such contradiction of sinners against himself, lest ye be wearied and faint in your minds.</u>" (Heb. 12:1-3)

The reality is that the Christian walk with God is not the low road of the world which leads nowhere, you will die in your sins. The high road leads against the beliefs and customs of a blind world. What is faith? Looking unto a heavenly destination, following the

Lord with the time you have on this earth and duration of your days. You might experience such:

- As Moses – the hardness of the way; leading an unruly people
- As Paul – the difficulty of the task; preaching to a new world
- As Joseph – the prosperity of the wicked; he rose above and God turned the tables in his favor
- As the disciples – the delay of the fulfillment and desires; the spreading of the gospel

If any of these servants were asked if they regret following God even against all contradiction, what would the answer be? Can you look back on your life and say, "I have made mistakes"? Most importantly, can you look ahead and say, "in spite of my past, I will have a better future in listening to God, obeying his word, abhorring that which is evil and sinful and cleaving to that which is good"? "I press toward the mark for the prize of the high calling of God in Christ Jesus." (Phil. 3:14)

Take the High Road
Doing the Right Thing

Chapter Six

Who Shall Deliver Me?

One of the worst things in this life is being caught in the middle. Two people are arguing or trying to decide something, and when you are asked your opinion, it forces you to choose a side.

When a person accepts Christ as Savior, the Holy Spirit comes to dwell in him/her for the rest of their life. Before you were saved, you didn't consider yourself a bad person, just a person who wanted to do what you wanted. "Leave me alone with all that religion," "who are you to judge;" these are statements made by someone hopelessly lost in their sins with no concern of eternity.

Everyone has a conscious whether saved or not, but that conscious that goes un-regenerated by the Holy Spirit will endure some of the most vile, immoral, or evil thoughts without concern of how low and depraved it has become. What I am saying is that there is a bottom that many people hit before they start realizing how low and miserable they have become. What is lower than the bottom, depression or death? A saying that has rung true throughout the years is this; "some people have to land flat on their back before they look up." When you have ended up in the hospital and you know you are captive in that bed, some will take that time to reflect on their life.

The undeniable truth is that everyone has a voice inside that speaks to them, whether in correction or pleasure of sin. The apostle Paul fought with himself to do the right thing. "For that which I do I allow not: for what I would, that do I not; but what I hate, that do I." (Rom. 7:15) This man was trying to serve God, and he knew what to do, but his old self kept fighting him.

To Whom are You Listening?

"For I know that in me (that is, in my flesh,) dwelleth no good thing: for to will is present with me; but how to perform that which is good I find not." (Rom. 7:18) In other words, I find it difficult to do the right thing. Let's investigate this to understand why we fight ourselves.

1. You are a three part person – not two as it seems:

   a. body – flesh desiring all things to satisfy

   b. soul – the middle where the final decision is determined

   c. spirit – the controlling factor of the results

2. Before saved you acted with two parts:

   a. the spirit – consulted with the "spirit of man"

   (I Cor. 2:11)

    b. the body – if it feels good do it (dwelleth no good thing that profits)

3. When the Holy Spirit enters at Salvation:

    a. your spirit has become re-generated – the Paraclete has come to help

    b. the soul is the part of you that filters good or bad – stagnant before, flowing now with the "Mind of Christ," the inner man (I Cor. 2:16)

    c. the body will sin or not depending on who you have yielded to; the spirit of man or the Spirit of God (Rom. 6:16)

    d. understand that the devil didn't concern himself much with an unsaved, blind, hell-bound sinner, but now you have chosen who's side you are on, and he will not give up trying to appeal to your flesh (body).

The worst thing in the devil's mind is to see any one glorifying God. It is a matter of who you really want to win. Paul didn't consider winning when the flesh had its way; "O wretched man that I am! who shall deliver me from the body of this death?" (Rom. 7:24)

Who Will Win?

    The victory only comes when the decision is made to serve Christ, with the <u>mind</u> of Christ. The soul consists of the <u>mind</u>, <u>will</u>, and <u>emotions</u> of a person and all decisions become manifest from the soul. "I thank God through Jesus Christ our Lord. So then with the mind I myself serve the law of God; but with the flesh the law of sin." (Rom. 7:25)

Jesus was "tempted in all like we;" according to Hebrews 4:15. So he does understand our struggles with sin. It has been said in the story of the black dog and the white dog of which one will win in a fighting match. The first day, everyone gathered around the ring to see these dogs face off. The white dog comes out all happy and wagging his tail, and the black dog comes out all growling and ferocious. Everyone bets on the black dog to win. Sure enough, that's exactly what happened, the black dog pinned the white dog down by the neck and it was over. The owner lost a lot of money. The next week, everyone gathered again at the dog fight eagerly to bet again on the black dog. Here comes the happy dog wagging his tail looking playful. Here comes the ferocious black dog, and they turned them loose to fight. The black dog jumped on the white dog biting him on the neck trying to pin him down to the ground, and as soon as the white dog went down, he rolled over and got a good bite-hold on the black dog, overpowering him as the black dog went down for the count. Everyone there had bet more on the black dog to win and lost all their money. They asked the owner after this unbelievable match why the mean black dog couldn't win. He said it is simple; if he wants the black dog to win, he feeds him more than the white dog, and if he wants the white dog to win, he will feed him more than the black dog. Moral of the story; which one you feed more, gets the victory.

Grace and Mercy

But, I want to be spiritual! I want to serve God and stay victorious. "For I delight in the law of God after the inward man: But I see another law in my members, warring against the law of my mind, and bringing me into captivity to the law of sin which is in my members." (Rom. 7:22-23) The book of Hebrews 4:16 tells us, "Let us therefore come boldly unto the throne of grace, that we may obtain mercy, and find grace to help in time of need."

As the prodigal son made his decision to leave home, strike out on his own, and be his own man, you can do what you want and find yourself in "want". You might have heard the popular statement today; "The heart wants what it wants." This can be one of the most destructive avenues introduced as a license to sin or live any lifestyle regardless of the consequences. The unbeliever beware, because you have no Holy guide. You will make wrong decisions, God knows; "The heart is deceitful above all things, and desperately wicked: who can know it?" (Jer. 17:9)

So, the prodigal went off and took his journey into a far country, "<u>and there wasted his substance with riotous living.</u>" (Luke 15:13) "And when he had spent all, there arose a mighty famine in that land; <u>and he began to be in</u> want. And he went and joined himself to a citizen of that country; and he sent him into his fields to feed swine. And he would fain have filled his belly with the husks that the swine did eat: and no man gave unto him." (Luke 15:14-16)

Sin will take you farther than you want to go, keep you longer than you want to stay, and cost you more than you want to pay.

A person knows when they have taken the low road, when they hit the bottom. There are "pleasures of sin for a season," (Heb.11:25), but when that season is over, then what? Notice in verse fifteen of Luke 15, that he had joined himself to a citizen; looks like a farmer, feeding the pigs. One would assume that he probably slept with them also. For a Jewish boy, this is degradation and humiliation to feed and dwell with these swine.

Who knew there would be a famine that would affect me so drastically? We can act like the victim for only so long, and finally realize that the changes need to be made to get back on track with God. This fellow left his home selfish and demanding, but returned with a humble prayer, "I will arise and go to my father, and will say unto him, Father, I have sinned against heaven, and before thee, And am no more worthy to be called thy son: make me as one of thy hired servants." (Luke 15:18-19)

God Knows our Situation

Desperation is a curious thing. One is forced in a direction one didn't intend to go. The question here is that would this young man have returned to his father if the money had not run out? You would think sooner or later, maybe as a visitor or at a family gathering. We can humbly come back to the Father in heaven with our head bowed, upon our knees, ready to accept orders for a new beginning, with new hope, for a new life. How much are we still willing to let God lead and how much is still in our mind to act out on our own?

Psalm 139 has proven to be one of the most revealing chapters of baring one's soul to an Almighty creator, acknowledging that God knows everything about us. You might be really messed up, you might not be thinking straight, you think you are too complicated to start out and not trustworthy of God's love; but, is there anything impossible for God?

"O Lord, thou hast searched me, and known me. Thou knowest my downsitting and mine uprising, thou understandest my thought afar off. Thou compassest my path and my lying down, and art acquainted with all my ways. For there is not a word in my tongue, but, lo, O Lord, thou knowest it altogether." (Psa. 139:1-4)

If you are not close to God, who moved? Returning to him is in your heart after a few hard lessons apart from him. He knows what it will take to get your life straight once again, what you need to do to draw closer to him, but the decisions will be left to you. The winnowing of wheat took tossing the wheat into the air, and the hull and chaff would separate, as Gideon did. Jesus told Peter that the devil hath desired to have you and sift you as wheat and he would deny Christ three times before the cock crows. (Luke 22:31,34)

I will not be able to escape your grace and mercy when I yield my life over to you. "Whither shall I go from thy spirit? or whither shall I flee from thy presence? If I ascend up into heaven, thou art there: if I make my bed in hell, behold, thou art there. If I take the wings of the morning, and dwell in the uttermost parts of the sea; Even there shall thy hand lead me, and thy right hand shall hold me. If I say, Surely the darkness shall cover me; even the night shall be light about me. Yea, the darkness hideth not from thee; but the night shineth as the day: the darkness and the light are both alike to thee. For thou hast possessed my reins: thou hast covered me in my mother's womb. I will praise thee; for I am fearfully and wonderfully made: marvelous are thy works; and that my soul knoweth right well." (Psa. 139:7-14)

Wisdom From on High

There is no false security with the Lord as the kings and the rulers of the earth take counsel to make their own way stand in the sight of Almighty God. Psalm 2:4 says, "He that sitteth in the heavens shall laugh: the Lord shall have them in <u>derision</u>." Which means they as worried kings shall <u>stammer</u>. This is a great lesson for the Christian that is <u>not</u> totally sold out or yielded completely to the Lord. "He that is not with me is against me: and he that gathereth not with me scattereth." (Luke 11:23)

There is not a perfect person alive; Jesus soley took that position. David was wise in Psalm 139:16 when he wrote, "Thine eyes did see my substance, yet being unperfect; and in thy book all my members were written, which in continuance were fashioned, when as yet there was none of them." This wisdom carries on in the present for everyone to learn who we are, what are your weaknesses, how you can overcome each with the hand of God on you.

"To confess you were wrong yesterday makes you a little wiser today." -- C.H. Spurgeon

"Can God give a straight blow with a crooked stick...?" -- Corrie Ten Boom

The Inward Man

Your body has to do what your mind tells it to. How much does the Law of God mean to you? Romans 7:22, "For I delight in the law of God after the inward man." You can be going through the motions of serving God, but you are misdirected. Saul of Tarsus, a rabbi of well-known tenacity, had a great zeal for serving God.

At the stoning of Stephen in Acts 7, he witnessed how one man's convictions led him to his death. How wrong he thought these Christians were to teach and preach this blasphemy against the Law of God, that he learned so well.

The inward man of Saul, soon to be Paul, was totally committed to wipe out this new way. "As for Saul, he made havock of the church, entering into every house, and haling men and women committed them to prison. Therefore they that were scattered abroad went every where preaching the word." (Acts 8:3-4) He delighted to do this; his inward man was motivated to accomplish his plan. "For as he thinketh in his heart, so is he…" (Prov. 23:7)

Ralph Waldo Emerson quoted, "A man is what he thinks about all day." Thomas Edison had only three months of formal schooling, but he changed the world. He had "<u>An inward driven motivation to fulfill a desired action</u>." Was Stephen wrong with his convictions, as all the other early Christians, or Saul with his convictions?

Carrying out his mission in Acts chapter 9, we read, "And Saul, yet breathing out threatenings and slaughter against the disciples of the Lord, went unto the high priest, And desired of him letters to Damascus to the synagogues, that if he found any of this way, whether they were men or women, he might bring them bound unto Jerusalem. And as he journeyed, he came near Damascus: and suddenly there shined round about him a light from heaven: And he fell to the earth, and he heard a voice saying unto him, Saul, Saul, why persecutest thou me? And he said, Who art thou, Lord? And the Lord said, I am Jesus whom thou persecutest: it is hard for thee to kick against the pricks. And he trembling and astonished said, Lord, what wilt thou have me to do? And the Lord said unto him, Arise, and go into the city, and it shall be told thee what thou must do." (Acts 9:1-6)

How could God use a man that persecuted Christians? How could the prodigal son's father take him back? Remember he knows you and he is able to see the potential in you. The inward man if not illuminated by the Spirit of God, will soon find a dead end as Saul did on the road to Damascus. Jesus had to intervene and stop this man from going any further. "The mind of a man is the battleground on which every moral and spiritual battle is fought." -- J. Oswald Sanders

"Search me, O God, and know my heart: try me, and know my thoughts: And see if there be any wicked way in me, and lead me in the way everlasting." (Psa. 139:23-24)

Testing

Nobody likes to go through testing, especially from the Lord, but somewhere in your inward person, you know it is the right thing to do. "For whom the Lord loveth he chasteneth, and scourageth every son whom he receiveth." (Heb.12:6) "Now no chastening for the present seemeth to be joyous, but grievous: nevertheless afterward it yieldeth the peaceable fruit of righteousness unto them which are exercised thereby. Wherefore lift up the hands which hang down, and the feeble knees; And make straight paths for your feet, lest that which is lame be turned out of the way; but let it rather be healed. Follow peace with all men, and holiness, without which no man shall see the Lord." (Heb. 12:11-14)

Isn't it good to have a teacher who wants you to pass?

The teacher in your past that wanted you to succeed is the most memorable. Life is our choice, healing has to take place, yielding to the master is wise. "Furthermore we have had fathers of our flesh which corrected us, and we gave them reverence: shall we not much rather be in subjection unto the Father of spirits, and live?" (Heb. 12:9) If a person runs from God, he has treated his grace with total disrespect and ungratefulness. "Looking diligently lest any man fail of the grace of God; lest any root of bitterness springing up trouble you, and thereby many be defiled; Lest there be any fornicator, or profane person, as Esau, who for one morsel of meat sold his birthright." (Heb.12:15-16) Our sins of selfish negligence fly in the face of a Holy God. The attitude of "turn your head, God, I am going to sin because I want to and know you will forgive me anyways," puts your salvation in a question of worth. Knowing that Jesus died so that we can live has to stay in our heart and bring obedience to our souls. "Casting down imaginations, and every high thing that exalteth itself against the knowledge of God, and bringing into captivity every thought to the obedience of Christ." (II Cor. 10:5)

We can learn from a wonderful illustration of an old wise man who lived on the mountain, that everyone went to for advice and counsel with their problems, and he always knew the answer. One day, two boys decided to try and trick the old man. One boy caught a bird and held it tightly in his hand behind his back. They proceeded to knock on the old wise man's door, and he came out to see them. The resentful teenage boy asked him a question, "can you guess what I have caught?" The wise old man said a bird. The boy planned to ask him next if the bird was dead or alive. If he says it is dead, he would let it fly away. And if he says it is alive, he would squeeze the life out of it and present a dead bird and this old wise man would fail. "So, old man, what have I caught?" He said, "it is a bird." "But now tell me, is it alive or dead?" The wise old man paused for a moment and looked into his eyes, and replied, "what you will it to be, it will be."

How does the story end? Will the bird remain alive, or will it die? It is up to you. How will you treat your free will to choose? "For the law of the Spirit of life in Christ Jesus hath made me free from the law of sin and death." (Rom. 8:2)

Take the High Road
Doing the Right Thing
Chapter Seven
Do Not Lust

How can a person conquer lust? How does God see the severity of lust in a Christian's life? These are two questions that have challenged even the most faithful. Matthew records Jesus saying, "But I say unto you, That whosoever looketh on a woman to lust after her hath committed adultery with her already in his heart." (Mat. 5:28) This sounds like the act of adultery doesn't need to be performed by the body, but the flesh is still at fault.

Jesus goes on to say, "And if the right eye offend thee, pluck it out, and cast it from thee: for it is profitable for thee that one of thy members should perish, and not that thy whole body should be cast into hell. And if thy right hand offend thee, cut it off, and cast it from thee: for it is profitable for thee that one of thy members should perish, and not that thy whole body should be cast into hell." (Mat.5:29-30) Does the Lord want people to live this life with body parts missing because of the lust of the heart?

A cement ceiling collapsed on a woman as she entered a building, and she lied there with her two legs trapped under a large slab. Paramedics arrived to find her bleeding severely and explained to her that they would have to cut off her legs or she would die. Bleed to death or consent to amputation were her only choices. What would you do? Of course, anyone would want to live.

It is unthinkable that a rational person would pluck out his own eye for lust after another. But what is the point that Jesus is making here? The changing of the heart is required. The penalty for sin is death, but can you rationalize saving your soul by losing members of the body? The law might require a thief to lose his hand or a person that commits adultery to be stoned, but what is the penalty for a sinful, lustful heart? Repent and accept that Christ will save you from an eternity in hell. If you don't conquer lust, it will conquer you.

Spiritual Light

The eye is figurative here, and Jesus continues the thought of the eye in chapter six of Matthew, "The light of the body is the eye: if therefore thine eye be single, thy whole body shall be full of light. But if thine eye be evil, thy whole body shall be full of darkness. If therefore the light that is in thee be darkness, how great is that darkness!" (Mat. 6:22-23)

The lusting of the eyes is the greatest delusion because of:

1. Spiritual immorality – tempted to lust, (James 1:14)

2. Blindness to reality – can't live to yourself, (Romans 14:7-8)

3. Constant self-offense - try to train your focus, (Matthew 5:29)

- If thy right eye "offend" thee, pluck it out. The word for offend in the Greek is, "skandalizo," to entrap; where we get the English word, "scandal."

Jesus' choice words referring to the "right hand" and "right eye" significantly mean that whatever the right eye desires, the right hand will act it out. What we look for, we see, and this influences our heart and the flesh will act upon it.

Going back to the three part person:

1. The spirit – pneuma – influenced by God or Satan; who you are listening to

2. The soul – psuche – influenced by the Spirit; mind, will, and emotions

3. The body – soma – influenced by the soul; the body will sin

Our own worst enemy is our self. Lust is a willful violation originating by Satan, fed to your mind, will, and emotions, and acted out by you. Shall we keep our eyes focused on the Lord and not on the things of this life? "Keep thy heart with all diligence; for out of it are the issues of life. Put away from thee a froward mouth, and perverse lips put far from thee. Let thine eyes look right on, and let thine eyelids look straight before thee. Ponder the path of thy feet, and let all thy ways be established. Turn not to the right hand nor to the left: remove thy foot from evil." (Prov. 4:23-27)

A Spiritual Comparison

Look at the lives of two men, both used by God to do mighty acts on earth, but their spiritual lives were very different one from the other. Samson and Daniel are prominent figures of the Old testament that are recorded for our benefit.

- Samson rejected God's Law on marriage and ended up losing his supernatural strength because of a heathen woman.
- Daniel decided to follow the Law of God even though it may have cost him his life, refusing authority and publicly praying three times daily.
- Samson had his eyes and mind on the ladies and demanded his parents to help him fulfill his lust.
- Daniel had his eyes and mind on the Lord with spiritual matters and spiritual visions.
- Samson refused to follow his childhood training, he was rebellious.
- Daniel followed his childhood training and brought glory to God and his people.
- Samson's physical lust and appetite resulted in being blinded, being enslaved, and brought his death.

- Daniel had self- control over lust and physical appetites and God honored him at the lion's den and in the kingdom.

Compare Your Old Self with Your New Self

Romans 12:1 says to, "...present your bodies a living sacrifice, holy, acceptable unto God, which is your reasonable service." To do this justifying act, you will need to follow the instructions of verse 2 of this chapter, "And be not conformed to this world: but be ye transformed by the <u>renewing</u> of your mind, that ye may <u>prove</u> what is that good, and acceptable, and perfect, will of God." To "renew" your mind, "anakainosis" in the Greek, means a "renovation" needs to take place. Not the same old you, but a brand new person with new thoughts. That you may "prove" what is acceptable to God is a big order indeed. "Dokinazo" in the Greek, means to examine, discern, try; and God can see right through the falsehoods.

I have always lived by the motto; "plan your work, then work your plan." This is the mentality here, like remodeling a house.

- ➢ Carefully write down a list of everything that needs work.
- ➢ Start one by one to conquer the areas with the least temptations.
- ➢ Realize that you are faced with the sin that "so easily besets" you; the enemy will fight you.

> Present yourself humbly before God, and let the Holy Spirit guide you to stand against the whiles of the devil – (Armor of God, Eph. 6).
> Constant renewing on a daily basis by prayer and the washing of God's word; pray, read, and memorize the Bible.
> Take an assessment of what your new renovation looks like now. Thank God for these victories.
> Determine to serve the Lord with this renewed spiritual strength and wisdom.

"But what things were gain to me, those I counted loss for Christ. Yea doubtless, and I counted all things but loss for the excellency of the knowledge of Christ Jesus my Lord: for whom I have suffered the loss of all things, and do count them but dung, that I may win Christ." (Phil. 3:7-8)

Lust Lingers

Solomon was a man that experienced many areas of self-fulfillment and found it all to be futile and a waste of time. Even the most devout Christian can fall prey to lust unintentionally. "Can a man take fire in his bosom, and his clothes not be burned?" (Prov. 6:27) The most honorable, God-serving man, had a ministry of rescuing people from alcohol addiction. He could go into a bar and talk to people about the Lord to bring them to salvation, then try to lead them down the right path. How wise would it be for a man who has had an alcohol problem to do this type of ministry? "Can one go upon hot coals, and his feet not be burned?" (Prov. 6:28) The mind can conjure up your senses to remember your favorite song or your favorite drink to start the temptation engine and lead to lust, then to sin. (Jam. 1:14-15) I know Christians that can get around drinking at a ballgame and taste it even though they have not had one sip.

Lust lingers about in this unrighteous and froward society; where you go, what you hear, and what you see will have a diverse impact on the unprepared Christian. "Be sober, be vigilant; because your adversary the devil, as a roaring lion, walketh about, seeking whom he may devour: whom resist steadfast in the faith, knowing that the same afflictions are accomplished in your brethren that are in the world. But the God of all grace, who hath called us unto his eternal glory by Christ Jesus, after that ye have suffered a while, make you perfect, stablish, strengthen, settle you." (I Pet. 5:8-10)

Friends

Friends become a touchy subject to those who are trying to change and commit their ways unto the Lord. It has been said that there are two kinds of people in this world-- "the saved and the lost." This is a true statement, but there is a third type of person that falls in between. This person is saved, but can be considered as a "carnal Christian;" that is to say, a person that enjoys the things of the flesh and goes along with everyone, but his spirituality is shallow. Have you ever looked into a pool of water where gold fish are swimming and discovered a white fish? The gold fish are your friends and the white one that stands out is you. Job's friends thought he needed reproving and counsel, when all along, he needed nothing but comfort and understanding. He was being tested and refined by God to the very core of his being and none of his friends could understand this.

There are unsaved friends that we need to eventually separate ourselves from, but some are saved and have no diligence for seeking the Lord. "Be not deceived: evil communications corrupt good manners. Awake to righteousness, and sin not; for some have not the knowledge of God: I speak this to your shame." (I Cor. 15:33-34)

Satisfaction of the Soul

The soul has an appetite that is hard to satisfy. "All the labour of man is for his mouth, and yet the appetite is not filled." (Eccl. 6:7) The flesh has an insatiable drive that controls a person, even if he has wisdom to resist. Why would a person sell his birthright for a bowl of stew? I think Esau knew that this stew was a temporary fix, but he said, "I am at the point to die" (Gen. 25:32)

Jesus confronted the woman of Samaria at the well in John chapter four, "…whosoever drinketh of this water shall thirst again: But whosoever drinketh of the water that I shall give him shall never thirst; but the water that I shall give him shall be in him a well of water springing up into everlasting life." (John 4:13-14)

The difference between the unsaved and the believer is that the unsaved have no resistance of the flesh. Some strong-willed people can stop fleshly vices, lose weight, exercise that old body into shape, and appear that they have full control. The saved are faced with all the same physical challenges, but have the spiritual strength that only God can give to resist the flesh, teach, and satisfy the soul's desires. "And the Lord shall guide thee continually, and satisfy thy soul in drought, and make fat thy bones: and thou shalt be like a watered garden, and like a spring of water, whose waters fail not." (Isa. 58:11)

The trials of Job came to a conclusion in God's favor. He proved himself to be a worthy servant. Yes, he went through every feeling and dismay of human emotions through his trials. But when he came to himself, he gave God the blessing. "I know that thou canst do every thing, and that no thought can be withholden from thee. Who is he that hideth counsel without knowledge? therefore have I uttered that I understood not; things too wonderful for me, which I knew not." (Job 42:2-3)

How can I know peace? When we sin, there is no peace. Lust uncontrolled brings unrest and guilt to our lives. The Christian is unable to walk with God with the inner peace. I John 1:9, "If we confess our sins, he is faithful and just to forgive us our sins, and to cleanse us from all unrighteousness." This is the Christian's bar of soap, meaning, we allow lust and sin knowing God will forgive and cleanse us back to fellowship with him. In all the while, this roller coaster is not a true walk with God. There is never peace with this arrangement.

Experience can bring wisdom to the person that acknowledges that they have this kind of relationship with God. "When wisdom entereth into thine heart, and knowledge is pleasant unto thy soul; Discretion shall preserve thee, understanding shall keep thee." (Prov. 2:10-11) You will find that it is hard to turn away from your weaknesses that cause you to lust, but the confirmation of the Spirit within you make it worth it. Only then can you start to grow fruits of the Spirit, genuine and in truth.

"But the fruit of the Spirit is love, joy, peace, longsuffering, gentleness, goodness, faith, meekness, temperance: against such there is no law. And they that are Christ's have crucified the flesh with the affections and lusts. If we live in the Spirit, let us also walk in the Spirit." (Gal. 5:22-25)

Take the High Road
Doing the Right Thing

Chapter Eight
Our Rock of Offence

It is human nature to cling to the past, to cling to our old ways and feel entitled to live the good life. The children of Israel were slaves for four hundred years in Egypt, then the deliverer finally came out from among the people. Why were the people enslaved in Egypt? God promised a mighty nation when Joseph was still alive; and now he is dead and a new king has arrived that did not know Joseph. "And the children of Israel were fruitful, and increased abundantly, and multiplied, and waxed exceeding mighty; and the land was filled with them. Now there arose up a new king over Egypt, which knew not Joseph. And he said unto his people, Behold, the people of the children of Israel are more and mightier than we: come on, let us deal wisely with them; lest they multiply, and it come to pass, that, when there falleth out any war, they join also unto our enemies, and fight against us, and so get them up out of the land. Therefore they did set over them taskmasters to afflict them with their burdens. And they built for Pharaoh treasure cities, Pithom and Raamses. <u>But the more they afflicted them, the more they multiplied and</u>

grew. And they were grieved because of the children of Israel." (Ex. 1:7-12)

This Pharaoh had the mind to bring God's people under his power and complete authority. But how can you overtake anything that God owns? Interfering in God's plan is useless unless God allows it. The children of Israel were blessed by God, not by this wicked king. You see how these people were a thorn in the flesh for this new ruler. What could he do with them that God could not undo because he has a bigger plan? They have become a stumbling block for him, which means, he has adopted an attitude of sinful, destructive behavior. A rock of offence that the world doesn't know how to handle.

Christianity has flourished among the nations by the hand of God and by the faith of his people. Peter addresses this irony in his first epistle, "To whom coming, as unto a living stone, disallowed indeed of men, but chosen of God, and precious, Ye also, as lively stones, are built up a spiritual house, an holy priesthood, to offer up spiritual sacrifices, acceptable to God by Jesus Christ. Wherefore also it is contained in the scripture, Behold, I lay in Sion a chief corner stone, elect, precious: and he that believeth on him shall not be confounded. Unto you therefore which believe he is precious: but unto them which be disobedient, the stone which the builders disallowed, the same is made the head of the corner. And a stone of stumbling, and a rock of offence, even to them which stumble at the word, being disobedient: whereunto also they were appointed. But ye are a chosen generation, a royal priesthood, an holy nation, a peculiar people; that ye should shew forth the praises of him who hath called you out of darkness into his marvellous light." (I Pet. 2:4-9)

Jesus has become the rock of offence to the unbelieving world. What can you do about Jesus when his followers are ever-present? No doubt that God has a plan for the world and the Christian. "The fool hath said in his heart, There is no God." (Psa. 53:1) All Christians agree on this undeniable fact that God exists, Jesus gave his life for yours, and we should walk by faith.

So here is a people that were led out of the land of bondage to journey to the land of promise. The question needs to be asked first, who is ready for the journey? We are all on this journey of faith the moment we accepted Jesus Christ as our savior. Will there be any obstacles to overcome on this journey? And what will it take to endure and not give up?

Test of Faith

Arriving at Rephidim after a long journey through the wilderness, they found that there was no water there. The people began to chide Moses. They murmured and complained intensely to the point of almost stoning him. "And Moses cried unto the Lord, saying, What shall I do unto this people? they be almost ready to stone me. And the Lord said unto Moses, Go on before the people, and take with thee of the elders of Israel;

and thy rod, wherewith thou smotest the river, take in thine hand, and go. Behold, I will stand before thee there upon the rock in Horeb; and thou shalt smite the rock, and there shall come water out of it, that the people may drink. And Moses did so in the sight of the elders of Israel." (Ex. 17:4-6)

When tried in the most adverse circumstance on your journey of faith, should a people turn from a happy, blessed, fruitful, life to the point of hostility? If this is the Christian's attitude of walking by faith with the Lord, Christianity itself has become a rock of offence. When a child doesn't get their way, they become upset and angry. When the walk with God gets challenging, shall we turn on God? "And he called the name of the place Massah, and Meribah, because of the chiding of the children of Israel, <u>and because they tempted the Lord, saying, Is the Lord among us, or not?</u>" (Ex. 17:7)

God Can Shape You

We live in such a religious society that if this church doesn't fit your views and opinions, just go find another one. I will guarantee that you will be able to find the most watered down version of Christianity out there and the most rigorous form of traditional church. If the preacher steps on your toes, or if you leave the service convicted of sin, or pressed to make a life-changing decision, by all means, evacuate. This is the norm of people today. You will find believers that share this attitude of never being satisfied, always searching to fill that desire for more out of their walk with God, because they don't have the courage to let God work and shape their lives as he sees fit, not their comfortable version. If church gets too intense, start going occasionally instead of faithfully. What did Jesus do to offend you?

Moses was called the deliverer because of the bondage of this greatly oppressed people. The attitude of the children of Israel as they left Egypt was one of hope and happiness, starting out on a new beginning with the promise from God with them. The same thing has happened in the Christian's life; started as delivered from sin at salvation, then started walking in an uncertain future with assurance that the Lord is leading and providing. Do we ever stop needing the Lord to lead and provide? How could Jesus ever become our stumbling block? He is the rock that was smitten that we may drink of eternal life freely. Smitten for our benefit, the just for the unjust.

Observe these facts:
- Supply was abundant – over 2 million people drank from the rock.
- Supply was lasting – they drank of the stream until they reached the promised-land.
- In the presence of the Elders – these men stayed skeptical then of God, and later, their descendants would pay Judas to betray Jesus Christ.
- Jesus gives the water of life freely – hanging on the cross, he was pierced in the side and water and blood came gushing out to cleanse and satisfy the thirsty soul.

My Rock

"Truly my soul waiteth upon God: from him cometh my salvation. He only is my rock and my salvation; he is my defence; I shall not be greatly moved." (Psa. 62:1-2) What can we accomplish through our own strength? We are shifty, we choose vanity, we need an anchor. We can't save ourselves and we are broken down. "...ye shall be slain all of you: as a bowing wall shall be, and as a tottering fence." (Psa. 62:3) Not steady, corrupt as an old wall or an old bridge that has become unsafe to cross. Paul was an exceptional man because after he got saved, he did not desire the things of this world nor the things of the flesh. He found these things to be false and an annoyance to his Christianity. He wrote about his new outlook on life and new goal to the Philippian church while he was imprisoned. How could this man have such a satisfied attitude and solitude of spirit? "For to me to live is Christ, and to die is gain. But if I live in the flesh, this is the fruit of my labour: yet what I shall choose I wot not. For I am in a strait betwixt two, having a desire to depart, and to be with Christ; which is far better." (Phil. 1:21-23) The ultimate gain is heaven; I know we can't see it now, but our indwelling Spirit which belongs to God, from God, and shall return to God, knows this quite well. When the world is closing in, your health has become an issue, your finances are shaky, the enemy is attacking on all sides, who has become the rock, fortress, and refuge? You can't shake a rock, it won't move. My stand is sure, I shall not be moved, he is my defense and salvation. "Nevertheless the foundation of God standeth sure, having this seal, The Lord knoweth them that are his. And, Let every one that nameth the name of Christ depart from iniquity." (II Tim. 2:19)

Jesus is Our Rock

Jesus has become that unmovable reality that man cannot manipulate, overcome, or overpower. Just because this world can't do anything about Jesus, they choose to not believe in him as the Jews have. "He came unto his own, and his own received him not." (John 1:11) Jesus admittedly came as a sword to divide people with truth. "Think not that I am come to send peace on earth: I came not to send peace, but a sword. For I am come to set a man at variance against his father, and the daughter against her mother, and the daughter in law against her mother in law. And a man's foes shall be they of his own household. He that loveth father or mother more than me is not worthy of me: and he that loveth son or daughter more than me is not worthy of me. <u>And he that taketh not his cross, and followeth after me, is not worthy of me. He that findeth his life shall lose it: and he that loseth his life for my sake shall find it.</u>" (Mat. 10:34-39) <u>Christianity cannot be a spectator event or something to add to your life, it must replace your old one.</u>

"If Christ is not all to you, He is nothing to you. He will never go into partnership as both Savior and man. If He be something, He must be everything, and if He be not everything, He is nothing to you." -- C.H. Spurgeon

Take the High Road
Doing the Right Thing

Chapter Nine
How is Your Speech?

Who is wise in their speech? What makes a person wise with their words? Is there an underlying restraint that makes them choose their words carefully? Job said; "...Behold, the fear of the Lord, that is wisdom; and to depart from evil is understanding." (Job 28:28) James, the brother of Jesus, devotes a whole chapter to this very sensitive matter in his epistle. "Who is a wise man and endued with knowledge among you? let him shew out of a good conversation his works with meekness of wisdom." (Jam. 3:13) Your actions and your words should prove God's word.

1. Jesus went as a sheep to the slaughter and opened not his mouth. (Isa. 53:7)
2. Daniel didn't curse and yell as they threw him into the lion's den.
3. Job didn't curse God and die as his wife suggested.
4. Abraham didn't question God's wisdom when he was asked to offer his son.

When you are determined to take the high road, the more challenging path with the Lord, you are yielding to the Holy Spirit, even in the most challenging circumstances. When John Huss, a preacher who dared to protest the authority of the pope in England, burned at the stake, he sang out loud until the flames blew in his face and choked him. When Stephen was being stoned, he cried with a loud voice, "…Lord, lay not this sin to their charge. And when he had said this, he fell asleep." (Acts 7:60) When Jesus hung on the cross, he said, "…Father, forgive them; for they know not what they do." (Luke 23:34)

Taming the Tongue

Why has the tongue become so difficult to tame? According to James 3:8-9, "But the tongue can no man tame; it is an unruly evil, full of deadly poison. Therewith bless we God, even the Father; and therewith curse we men, which are made after the similitude of God." But wait a minute, all these that went before us somehow used constraint. "Doth a fountain send forth at the same place sweet water and bitter?" (Jam. 3:11) Sometimes it is better to not say anything than to speak and reveal your knowledge and lack of understanding. "Some may think we are ignorant, but we open our mouths and remove all doubt." -- Abraham Lincoln

Heavenly Direction

You have had a long time to store up the things of the flesh in your heart, and these things are coming to the surface. There is a town that had a natural gas leak from a station where it was stored. Nobody knew this leak happened until the gas traveled underground for days into an available channel, then erupted from anywhere it could escape. Buildings caught fire, explosions caused deaths, and officials were puzzled about how all this was happening. For days they tried to put out a fire that was fed from underground, so that gave them the first clue that there was a deadly leak forcing this gas. Checking all the storage stations finally revealed this leak, but the damage had already occurred. People lost their lives, buildings were destroyed, and restoration took years.

The question has to be, what have you given to the Lord in repentance and asked him for understanding and wisdom for your condition? "For where envying and strife is, there is confusion and every evil work." (Jam. 3:16) "But I am not evil." But, what you carry inside can be used by the enemy and can bring a canker to your soul if you don't continually place these things under the blood to purify.

"But the wisdom that is from above is first pure, then peaceable, gentle, and easy to be intreated, full of mercy and good fruits, without partiality, and without hypocrisy." (Jam. 3:17)

The things that we keep inside will form our character and the heart will cry out. "Keep thy heart with all diligence; for out of it are the issues of life. Put away from thee a froward mouth, and perverse lips put far from thee." (Prov. 4:23-24) This challenge can only be met through the ever discerning coaching of the Holy Spirit.

A Marine billboard read, "Pain is weakness leaving the body." This character building will be strict but necessary for the believer. Before you were saved, the profanity and sinful thoughts flowed from your speech. Now you should be offended when you hear this type of language.

What are the things that are still in need of attention?

1. Bitterness – Hebrews 12:15, "…lest any root of bitterness springing up trouble you, and thereby many be defiled."
2. Pride – Proverbs 13:10, "Only by pride cometh contention."
3. Hatred – Proverbs 10:12, "Hatred stirreth up strifes: but love covereth all sins."
4. Anger – Proverbs 14:17, "He that is soon angry dealeth foolishly."
5. Covetousness – Hebrews 13:5, "Let your conversation be without covetousness; and be content with such things as ye have…"
6. Criticality – James 2:4, "Are ye not then partial in yourselves, and are become judges of evil thoughts?"

Power in the Tongue

What good can come from the tongue? What pleases God? The noblest thing is prayer, words from our hearts. "Pray without ceasing." (I Thess. 5:17) When we witness and share the gospel message, we encourage, we love, and lift up. Glorifying God is meant to be the result.

An Egyptian King once sent a sacrifice to his god and requested the priest to send back the best and worst part of the animal. He sent back the tongue representing both demands. The tongue has the power to do good or bad. It can give great harm as a deadly weapon to defame individuals, divide families, destroy churches, and deaden the gospel. "Even so the tongue is a little member, and boasteth great things. Behold, how great a matter a little fire kindleth!" (Jam. 3:5) It's the case of Mrs. O'Leary's cow starting the Great Chicago fire in 1871, killing 250 people, and destroying 17,400 buildings. One deadly slip and history is made.

Watch What You Say

Jesus pushes for a decision in Matthew 12:33-37, "Either make the tree good, and his fruit good; or else make the tree corrupt, and his fruit corrupt: for the tree is known by his fruit. O generation of vipers, how can ye, being evil, speak good things? for out of the abundance of the heart the mouth speaketh. A good man out of the good treasure of the heart bringeth forth good things: and an evil man out of the evil treasure bringeth forth evil things. But I say unto you, That every idle word that men shall speak, they shall give account thereof in the day of judgement. For by thy words thou shalt be justified, and by thy words thou shalt be condemned." Jesus knows our hearts will be defiled by our words, and he knows the spiritual condition of the person by what comes out of his mouth.

Taking the high road with God and doing the right thing will challenge one's self-control. When the Apostle Paul persecuted Christians as Saul of Tarsus, the Bible tells us that he had a hatred for Christians, in Acts 9:1, "And Saul, yet breathing out threatenings and slaughter against the disciples of the Lord, went unto the high priest." We are not told the words he used, but the condition of his heart is quite evident. But now we read in I Corinthians 9:27; "But I keep under my body, and bring it into subjection: lest that by any means, when I have preached to others, I myself should be a castaway."

What made the difference in Paul's life?
- When he accepted Christ, his heart changed.
- He cared about the salvation of people.
- He respected the authority of the Word of God.
- He knew the power of a misspoken word; the enemy twists things.
- The mission had to be fulfilled with a clean conscience.

Silence is Golden

"Blessed is the man who, having nothing to say, abstains from giving wordy evidence of the fact." -- George Elliot

Forgive me, Lord, for careless words, when hungry souls are near.

Words that are not of faith and love, heavy with care and fear;

Forgive me for the words withheld, for words that might have won,

A soul from darkened paths and sin, to follow thy dear son:

Words are such mighty things, dear Lord, may I so yield be,

That Christ, who spake as never man, may ever speak through me.

When there is nothing to say, say nothing. Jesus went quietly as a lamb to the slaughter according to Isaiah 53:7, "He was oppressed, and he was afflicted, yet he opened not his mouth: he is brought as a lamb to the slaughter…" What could he have said? He came with his mission in mind, responsibility taking precedence over every emotion, every temptation to set these persecutors straight.

I would rather say little than to think back on a conversation and regret some things I said. People choose to argue when saying nothing is the most responsible thing to do. Case in point: two people arguing with loud, angry voices, the phone rings, and one of them answers in a soft, loving voice to whoever is on the other end. "But if ye have bitter envying and strife in your hearts, glory not, and lie not against the truth." (Jam. 3:14) Can your bitterness become so deep that it can come between you and God?

There is no need to make apologies if you control what you say and the manner in which you say it. Like a dandelion blowing in the wind, can you go and collect all the seeds that blew off?

A woman spread lies about a preacher all over town. He confronted her about why she spread such falsehoods. What did he do to her? She being caught, apologized to him. He said, "I forgive you, but come with me." They went to the bell tower at the top of the church. He cut open a feather pillow and the feathers went every direction. He said, "When you can go and collect every feather, all the damage will be taken back." "A word sent forth from the lips cannot be brought back even with a chariot and six horses." -- Chinese Proverb

Heart Challenge

To control the tongue, one must control the heart. Nobody's perfect, but experience is wisdom. You may find that the best way to deal with issues that connect the heart with the tongue is two things:

1. Is what you are saying glorifying to God – encouragement, edifying, etc.
2. Mean what you say and say what you mean – no area of doubt and confusion.

"And whatsoever ye do, do it heartily, as to the Lord, and not unto men." (Col. 3:23) "...but let your yea be yea; and your nay, nay; lest ye fall into condemnation." (Jam. 5:12)

James concluded the third chapter with our challenge of discernment. Verses 16-18, "For where envying and strife is, there is confusion and every evil work. But the wisdom that is from above is first pure, then peaceable, gentle, and easy to be intreated, full of mercy and good fruits, without partiality, and without hypocrisy. And the fruit of righteousness is sown in peace to them that make peace."

Get away from the middle ground where confusion dwells, and take the high road with God. As verse 15 states three words; "<u>earthly, sensual, devilish,</u>" these are on the low road where the enemy wants you to stay. Then the wisdom of God (could even be translated as "<u>in Christ</u>") is where God wants you now and eternally.

Take the High Road
Doing the Right Thing
Chapter Ten
The Sin of Unbelief

Can we maintain our belief and come up short? The children of Israel worshipped God, kept his laws, and God delivered them out of Egypt. The children of Egypt wandered in the desert for forty years because of unbelief. The same as someone who claims to be a believer today and can go through the motions, but not see the promise of God in their life. The Bible uses the term, "rest," in the book of Hebrews; the Greek word, "katapausis," meaning "abide." "Let us therefore fear, lest, a promise being left us of entering into his <u>rest</u>, any of you should seem to come short of it." (Heb. 4:1)

Some will hear the same gospel message preached, but not be affected and go on about their business. In a church scenario, the umbrella of worship and organizational fellowship exists, but don't be fooled into thinking that everyone is held in belief though the unity seems good. Are there people in church that are not saved, but still present? "For unto us was the gospel preached, as well as unto them: but the word preached did not profit them, not being mixed with faith in them that heard it. For we which have believed do enter into rest, as he said, As I have sworn in my wrath, if they shall enter into my rest: although the works were finished from the foundation of the world." (Heb. 4:2-3)

What is obvious to the spiritual eye here is that God has made a predetermined blueprint, so to say, of the plan for the ages set at the beginning to carry through this present world unto eternity. "For he spake in a certain place of the seventh day on this wise, And God did rest the seventh day from all his works. And in this place again, If they shall enter into my rest. Seeing therefore it remaineth that <u>some</u> must enter therein, and they to whom it was first preached enter not in because of unbelief." (Heb. 4:4-6)

The Authority of Jesus

The unbelief of these Hebrews meant no entrance into the promised land, no rest. "For if Jesus had given them rest, then would he not afterward have spoken of another day. There remaineth therefore a rest to the people of God." (Heb. 4:8-9) The opportunity is very clear and needs to be a <u>definite decision</u> in a person's life. Get off the fence and make your stand clear, not in just word, but in deed also. "Let us labour therefore to enter into that, lest any man fall after the same example of unbelief." (Heb. 4:11)

We live in the world of second chances because of the finished work of Jesus Christ on the Cross. "Looking unto Jesus the author and finisher of our faith; who for the joy that was set before him endured the cross, despising the shame, and is set down at the right hand of the throne of God." (Heb. 12:2) We belong to Jesus in our faith. Whatever we do, wherever we go, he is ever present. If we sin, he is there to be our High Priest. "Seeing then that we have a great high priest, that is passed into the heavens, Jesus the Son of God, let us hold fast our profession." (Heb. 4:14)

Accept the fact that the Shepherd can look at his flock and know if not all his sheep are present. If we accept his sacrifice for our sins, we should accept his leading. Realize that the only way you will get to heaven is by Jesus Christ. Also, the only way you can survive this sinful world is to follow him on purpose. "Let us therefore come boldly unto the throne of grace, that we may obtain mercy, and find grace to help in time of need." (Heb. 4:16)

Battle of Unbelief

We can still battle with unbelief that leads to:

1. Wasted time – "Redeeming the time, because the days are evil." (Eph. 5:16) e.g. Israel's 40 year march in the desert, not heeding Noah until too late. Jesus said; "Follow me; and let the dead bury their dead." (Mat. 8:22)

2. Wasted efforts – "…the care of this world, and the deceitfulness of riches, choke the word, and he becometh unfruitful." (Mat. 13:22) "No servant can serve two masters: for either he will hate the one, and

love the other; or else he will hold to the one, and despise the other. Ye cannot serve God and mammon." (Luke 16:13)

3. A spiritual stalemate – we cannot be on strike when we are already so blessed; "And Elijah came unto all the people, and said, How long halt thee between two opinions? If the Lord be God, follow him: but if Baal, then follow him. And the people answered him not a word." (I Kings 18:21)

Walk After the Spirit

God has made us free in Christ Jesus. How easy is it to walk after the flesh and lose that freedom? All saved people are not condemned because of being "in Christ". "There is therefore now no condemnation to them which are in Christ Jesus, who walk not after the flesh, but after the Spirit." (Rom. 8:1) So if a Christian is not condemned, how can he lose his freedom? The answer is a most precarious one because even though the freedom from the flesh is present and the release from the bondage of sin is vicariously set in place, many still choose a path similar to the carnal minded. "For to be carnally minded is death: but to be spiritually minded is life and peace. Because the carnal mind is enmity against God: for it is not subject to the law of God, neither indeed can be. So then they that are in the flesh cannot please God." (Rom. 8:6-8)

The "flesh" and "carnal" are the same Greek word, "sarx," meaning external, human nature with its frailties and passions. This would make sense that once a person is born-again he/she has a human nature that is trumped by a divine nature (Holy Spirit) that comes to dwell forever. This new divine nature surpasses all the human tendencies to sin. When one still sins, he is reminded by the Holy Spirit that they just violated the union. This seems to be the age-old and world-wide dilemma of all time. I am not carnal but spiritual because of salvation, but I act like my flesh and its needs and desires take priority over the Spirit. Ephesians 5:29 states; "For no man ever yet hated his own flesh; but nourisheth and cherisheth it, even as the Lord the church."

The Flesh Profits Nothing

How much money is spent each year on casual comforts of the body? For example: hair products, make up; the average woman spends $4,000 per year. Clothes than can exceed thousands of dollars per year for both men and women. Exercise, diet, and all the programs of the world will never satisfy the spiritual desire. "For bodily exercise profiteth little: but godliness is profitable unto all things, having promise of life that now is, and of that which is to come." (I Tim. 4:8)

The truth is that anything of this world that doesn't penetrate to the spiritual sense of the person is of the flesh and not profitable. The word preached, the beautiful soul-stirring music, the heart-felt testimonies of a Christian are necessary for spiritual growth. The Bible says in I Corinthians 15:22; "For as in Adam all die, even so in Christ shall all be made alive." So this means I can be in Christ and remain alive. The union that Christ has with a believer is eternal whether you act carnal or not.

Spiritual Oneness

You can't change the fact that you are in the body, you dwell in your person, but the Holy Spirit has bonded you to Jesus Christ. This changes everything for your present outlook as well as the future. "I can do all things through Christ which strengtheneth me." (Phil. 4:13) Allowing anyone or anything to strengthen becomes the sin of unbelief that God can't fulfill his will and biblical promises in your life.

It is the most difficult thing as a strong-willed, decisive person to ask for strength and guidance, but realize that you are also receiving wisdom and power when you pray and include the Lord daily. "As ye have therefore received Christ Jesus the Lord, so walk ye in him: Rooted and built up in him, and stablished in the faith, as ye have been taught, abounding therein with thanksgiving. Beware lest any man spoil you through philosophy and vain deceit, after the tradition of men, after the rudiments of the world, and not after Christ. For in him dwelleth all the fulness of the Godhead bodily. And ye are complete in him, which is the head of all principality and power." (Col. 2:6-10)

<u>The sin of unbelief is not letting God lead even though Jesus is living inside the believer and has all power in heaven and earth.</u>

Love is the Proof

I love the Lord deep down inside, I want to follow and obey his word. How can I get close to God and stay there? I find myself messing things up and digging myself into a hole. People around me can't see what is going on inside, but God can. "Jesus said unto him, Thou shalt love the Lord thy God with all thy heart, and with all thy soul, and with all thy mind."(Matt. 22:37) The motives in which we do all these things are centered around this fact-- are you doing things for the right reason? What is your motive?

1. <u>I want to seek God</u> – to be a better person, or to please God?
2. <u>Commit to Bible study</u> – for God to bless me, or to learn more about God?
3. <u>Memorize and meditate on scripture</u> – to show how spiritual I am, or to make scripture a part of my thinking to make the right decisions?
4. <u>Overcome temptations</u> – to build my will, or to be fruitful for the glory of God?
5. <u>Fast and pray</u> – to lose weight and have better health, or to be more receptive to the leading of the Holy Spirit?
6. <u>Dedicate yourself to God's will</u> – to make up for the past, or to let God work through you in Christ?
7. <u>Give money</u> – God to bless my finances, or help meet the needs of God's work of the ministry?

Motives matter to God, and he knows your heart.

I Corinthians 3:13, "Every man's work shall be made manifest: for the day shall declare it, because it shall be revealed by fire; and the fire shall try every man's work of what sort it is."

The world pushes romance for couples, but God teaches love. What makes a man visit his wife in a nursing home every day? Is it love or obligation? Their marriage lasted 50 years, and she finally passed away. And, less than 6 months later he passed also. The heart can be attached to someone and when they are gone it is very difficult to move on. The same thing is true when you have a true relationship with the Lord. It is impossible to have a relationship with God and still not believe who he really is.

God loves us just the way we are, but too much to leave us the way we are. He can take ordinary people with ordinary ways to do extraordinary things. Would you just rather taste of his power or be connected to the source? Taste the water or have the well?

A mechanic was once asked, "why are wheel alignments so important?" He answered, "If you don't get your vehicle aligned, the front wheels want to go one way, and the back wheels want to go another way, and the vehicle will have its own inner struggle and lose power on its own." One direction at a time is the plan, not the human interpretation of the Holy Spirit.

"Nevertheless I have somewhat against thee, because thou hast left thy first love." (Rev. 2:4) John penned these words straight from the mouth of Jesus Christ about the condition of the church at Ephesus. Even though this church had labor and patience, it lacked the true love that it started with. As the serpent beguiled Eve in the Garden of Eden, this slow moving corruption moved into the church and the love for Christ waned away.

The very defect that Jesus saw in this great church has happened to most well-meaning Christians. The love has grown cold. "Though I speak with the tongues of men and of angels, and have not charity, I am become as sounding brass, or a tinkling cymbal." (I Cor. 13:1)

Love Comes From God

How can I keep this love growing strong? "Who shall separate us from the love of Christ? shall tribulation, or distress, or persecution, or famine, or nakedness, or peril, or sword?" (Rom. 8:35) Realize this love comes from God. "We love him, because he first loved us." (I John 4:19) Let's set the record straight. True love is not of this world, it is from God only through his Son, Jesus Christ.

"In this was manifested the love of God towards us, because that God sent his only begotten Son into the world, that we might live through him." (I John 4:9) Trying to muster up the Christian life on our own is futile. God will not accept it as we saw Cain's offering was unacceptable, and Abel's offering, by blood, was entreated and accepted by God. "Herein is love, not that we loved God, but that he loved us, and sent his Son to be the propitiation for our sins."(I John 4:10)

"Propitiation" in the Greek, "hilasmos," the "atonement," which in definition means reparation, compensation, payment, and restitution. The Lord knows how to heal and get our attention. He wants the world to accept his love shown to us by the cross and shed blood of Christ. And, to start a relationship with him, walking by faith, trusting that he knows how to save and lead our lives as long as we are alive on this earth.

The clear definition of unbelief is the absence of faith.

Paul states it like this in Romans 14:23, "...for whatsoever is not of faith is sin." The sin of unbelief will keep you from all that God offers you.

"Since the day Jesus died on the cross, was buried, and rose again, Satan has known he was fighting a losing battle, he could not overthrow God, he could not corrupt the entire human race. There is only one thing left that he can do against God, and that is to damn the unbeliever..." [4] (Oliver B. Greene)

---

[4] Oliver B. Greene, "Why Does the Devil Desire to Damn You?" The Gospel Hour, 1966, pg. 30

Take the High Road
Doing the Right Thing

Chapter Eleven
The High Cost of Low Living

There is an old expression, "Not all that glitters is gold." A person can look back on their life and wonder why they made the decisions that they had made. Why didn't I take that job, why didn't I go to college, why didn't I marry that person? Would life be different if we had made other choices?

We find in the book of Genesis chapter thirteen that Abraham and Lot, his nephew, dwelt together and God had blessed them so much that there was no room for all their herds and stock. "And Abram said unto Lot, Let there be no strife, I pray thee, between me and thee, and between my herdmen and thy herdmen; for we be brethren. Is not the whole land before thee? separate thyself, I pray thee, from me: if thou wilt take the left hand, then I will go to the right; or if thou depart to the right hand, then I will go to the left. And Lot lifted up his eyes, and beheld all the plain of Jordan, that it was well watered every where…" (Gen. 13:8-10)

The story goes that Lot separated all his people and belongings to pitch his tent toward Sodom. Abraham dwelled in the land of Canaan. We don't know if Lot knew the reputation of the wickedness of Sodom and Gomorrah or if he just wanted to dwell in the plains and live on the edge of the sin city; but the Bible tells us that he ended up in the city, as Abraham dwelled in the plains.

"And the Lord appeared unto him in the plains of Mamre: and he sat in the tent door in the heat of the day; And he lift up his eyes and looked, and, lo, three men stood by him: and when he saw them, he ran to meet them from the tent door, and bowed himself toward the ground." (Gen. 18:1-2) Something was going on to have these heavenly guests show up at Abraham's door. The chief visitor was Jehovah himself, "the Angel of the Lord," and Abraham soon recognized this.

"And the Lord said, Because the cry of Sodom and Gomorrah is great, and because their sin is very grievous; I will go down now, and see whether they have done altogether according to the cry of it, which is come unto me; and if not, I will know. And the men turned their faces from thence, and went toward Sodom: but Abraham stood yet before the Lord." (Gen. 18:20-22)

Bring Your Petition to God

Abraham knew his nephew Lot and all his family lived in Sodom and Gomorrah, and the appeal to the

Lord began for their lives. "And Abraham drew near, and said, Wilt thou also destroy the righteous with the wicked? Peradventure there be fifty righteous within the city: wilt thou also destroy and not spare the place for the fifty righteous that are therein?" (Gen. 18:23-24)

The Lord agreed to spare the city if there were fifty righteous. But, just to be on the safe side, Abraham humbly pleaded for forty-five, forty, thirty, twenty, ten righteous to be found; would the city be destroyed?

Here is a loving, protective man that cares for his relatives enough to bargain with God to save their lives. Meanwhile, one can only imagine all the sin and wickedness of the society in which Lot dwells. What happened to all these herds and possessions? He probably was still wealthy and a prominent resident of this place because he sat at the gate, according to Genesis 19:1. It is not a small matter to make the wrong choices in life and things start to get out of control.

How long do people stay in their addictions knowing the consequences are dangerous? But, nonetheless, tolerance of living against the wisdom of God will catch up to you. You do reap what you sow. "There is a way which seemeth right unto a man, but the end thereof are the ways of death." (Prov. 14:12) Why did God speak to Abraham and not to Lot?

Life Choices

What kind of life did Lot choose, and could God bless his decision? We find in Genesis fourteen that war broke out between four kings with five kings against Sodom and Gomorrah. "And they took Lot, Abram's brother's son, who dwelt in Sodom, and his goods, and departed." (Gen. 14:12) Abram rose up to defend Lot. "And when Abram heard that his brother was taken captive, he armed his trained servants, born in his own house, three hundred and eighteen, and pursued them unto Dan. And he divided himself against them, he and his servants, by night, and smote them, and pursued them unto Hobah, which is on the left hand of Damascus. And he brought back all the goods, and also brought again his brother Lot, and his goods, and the women also, and the people." (Gen. 14:14-16)

A person would think that after such an ordeal as this war, a person would not want to go back into Sodom and Gomorrah. God intervened here using Abram and his people as the rescue team. But, why do ones as Lot and the King of Sodom not turn to God?

"And Melchizedek king of Salem brought forth bread and wine: and he was the priest of the most high God. And he blessed him, and said, Blessed be Abram of the most high God, possessor of heaven and earth: And blessed be the most high God, which hath delivered thine enemies into thy hand. And he gave him tithes of all." (Gen. 14:18-20) All of this was done and known of all that the King of Sodom, too, wanted to reward Abram and his people by offering a booty of this war. But, Abram replied, "...I have lift up mine hand unto the Lord, the most high God, the possessor of heaven and earth, That I will not take from a thread even to a shoelatchet, and that I will not take any thing that is thine, lest thou shouldest say, I have made Abram rich." (Gen. 14:22-23)

One can see the character of Abram and how he gives God the glory for everything in his life. What could Lot possibly be thinking as he went back to Sodom and Gomorrah? But, we know the story's end and he does not have a clue that his decisions will turn out so seriously.

Righteous?

When people refuse to go to church and refuse to hear anything about Jesus and what he did to sacrifice for them, you can't help but wonder if they realize the seriousness of their decisions. I am sure Lot was thankful, but would you consider Lot to be a righteous man? I am sure there are many saved individuals that are living in a perverse lifestyle today and are convicted somewhat of this atmosphere. Lot was righteous living among these people. "For that righteous man dwelling among them, in seeing and hearing, vexed his righteous soul from day to day with their unlawful deeds." (II Pet. 2:8)

So now, the two angels from God are at the twin cities of Sodom and Gomorrah meeting Lot at the gate where this important man Lot sat. "...and Lot seeing them rose up to meet them; and he bowed himself with his face toward the ground; And he said, Behold now, my lords, turn in, I pray you, into your servant's house, and tarry all night, and wash your feet, and ye shall rise up early, and go your ways. And they said, Nay; but we will abide in the street all night. And he pressed upon them greatly; and they turned in unto him, and entered into his house; and he made them a feast, and did bake unleavened bread, and they did eat." (Gen. 19:1-3)

News travels fast when there are visitors because these two angels arrived in the evening and before they could finish their meal and lay down to rest; there are people from every area of town at Lot's door wanting to meet their visitors. "And they called unto Lot, and said unto him, Where are the men which came in to thee this night? bring them out unto us, that we may know them." (Gen. 19:5) The Hebrew word for "know" here is "yada," meaning, to get or have or take, also to recognize or acquaint. The expression seemed to warrant a fear into Lot because of his reply; "And said, I pray you, brethren, do not so wickedly. Behold now, I have two daughters which have not known man; let me, I pray you, bring them out unto you, and <u>do ye to them as is good in your eyes</u>: only unto these men do nothing; for therefore came they under the shadow of my roof." (Gen. 19:7-8)

Remember this saying, "Sin will take you farther than you want to go, keep you longer than you want to stay, and cost you more than you want to pay" Lot had obviously lost his testimony about God to everyone. These men were ready to break down the door to get what they wanted with no respect for Lot and his family. Criminal behavior is in our present world. As many today have lost their testimonies, the boundaries and limitations are blurred. You can't control the sin of others, you can't control their will and minds. The natural sinner according to Romans seven, is hard to control, "...for to will is present with me; but how to perform that which is good I find not." (Rom. 7:18)

A Texas couple started raising a lion cub. The cub was loveable, cute, and playful. They also had a baby in the house. One day they stepped out their door for a few seconds, and heard their baby crying, so they ran back into the house to find the lion cub had chewed three fingers off the baby.

Judgment

"Woe to the rebellious children, saith the Lord, that take counsel, but not of me; and that cover with a covering, but not of my spirit, that they may add sin to sin." (Isa. 30:1) "For they have sown the wind, and they shall reap the whirlwind..." (Hos. 8:7) Judgment is inevitable to those who blatantly refuse to acknowledge God, and his mercy.

"And when the morning arose, then the angels hastened Lot, saying, Arise, take thy wife, and thy two daughters, which are here; lest thou be consumed in the iniquity of the city." (Gen. 19:15)

Two things happened prior to this morning of reckoning:

1. The angels smote the perverted men at the door who tried to commit immoral acts with them, with blindness.

"...and sin, when it is finished, bringeth forth death." (Jam. 1:15)

2. The warnings to Lot's sons in law to flee the city because they will be destroyed. They just mocked him in sin and unbelief. "Be not deceived; God is not mocked: for whatsoever a man soweth, that shall he also reap." (Gal. 6:7)

They lingered, not wanting to leave their home and property. The angels had to pull them out of the city by the hand, and told them not to look back. "And it came to pass, when they had brought them forth abroad, that he said, Escape for thy life; look not behind thee, neither stay thou in all the plain; escape to the mountain, lest thou be consumed." (Gen. 19:17)

We began with Abraham pleading with God over at least ten righteous souls to dwell in Sodom and Gomorrah. Who we see that escaped this tragic situation, is Lot, his wife, and two daughters. It's funny how the bad habits and rebellious nature can follow you even after a strict warning. The angels gave them clear instruction to not look back. The logic in this is still not clear, but we can't always understand God, and we should always obey God.

Disobedience

"Then the Lord rained upon Sodom and upon Gomorrah brimstone and fire from the Lord out of heaven; And he overthrew those cities, and all the plain, and all the inhabitants of the cities, and that which grew upon the ground. But his wife looked back from behind him, and she became a pillar of salt." (Gen. 19:24-26) Lot lost his wife because of the longings for material things, so he and his two daughters escaped to a nearby city named Zoar. Another detail to point out is that they were told to flee to the mountain in verse 17, but again, Lot had an alternate plan.

Most likely Zoar would have been consumed because of the close proximity of the small town. The Bible does show that it is located near the Dead Sea. It is a miracle that they survived this judgment of God being so close to the destruction, but he and his two daughters ended up there.

You can take a person out of sin, but you can't take sin out of a person.

Lot's daughters now alone with him must have inherited the same sinful qualities of Lot. Their scheme was to get Lot drunk and take turns lying with him because there was no one else that would have them now, and to preserve their father's seed. "Thus were both the daughters of Lot with child by their father." (Gen. 19:36) They got what they wanted, but could God bless this sort of incestuous behavior?

"And the firstborn bare a son, and called his name Moab: the same is the father of the Moabites unto this day. And the younger, she also bare a son, and called his name Benammi: the same is the father of the children of Ammon unto this day." (Gen. 19:37-38)

Needless to say, these descendants of Lot and his two daughters were never close to Israel. The idolatry of both tribes and the animosity held between them and Israel were never settled. This should tell us that the wrong choices were made. God had a different plan, but they chose otherwise.

Godly Choices

Many will make choices good and bad over the period of their life. The bad choices can lead down the wrong road to destruction in the end. The good road can lead to God's will and blessing to victory in life. To examine the two lives of Abraham and Lot, we must realize that life isn't easy no matter which road you take. One may be hard, but the other is much harder. The low cost of living with God, letting God bless and protect, and the high cost of low living, taking risks, hoping God will bless and lead.

Abraham's road	**Lot's road**
good pasture land	property closed in, crime-infested
faithful followers	nobody would listen, sons in law mocked him
wealthy	wealth had to be guarded
peace	no peace, lived in fear
faith	no sign of faith or prayers

directed by God	cities destroyed, lived in mountain cave
victorious in life	no victory, lost it all, daughters bear adversaries

Lot started as a righteous man, but made bad choices. But according to II Peter, he was called "just."

"And delivered just Lot, vexed with the filthy conversation of the wicked: (For that righteous man dwelling among them, in seeing and hearing, vexed his righteous soul from day to day with their unlawful deeds;) The Lord knoweth how to deliver the godly out of temptations, and to reserve the unjust unto the day of judgment to be punished." (II Pet. 2:7-9)

Let God set you on the high road by powerfully obeying the Holy Spirit's instructions. Otherwise, you could suffer the "high cost of low living."

Take the High Road
Doing the Right Thing

Chapter Twelve
The Sin of Indifference

The dictionary defines the word "indifference" as the lack of interest, concern, apathy, etc. The Bible records the word "light," as "they made light of it," in Matthew 22:5; as Jesus told the parable of the marriage of the king's son. "Ameleo," in the Greek, to be careless, neglect, negligent, or not regard.

According to the Barna Research Group, there are people today that are "spiritual but not religious." There are those who don't claim any faith at all; they are 12% atheist, 30% agnostic, 58% unaffiliated. Among those that claim no faith are 34% that claim to not identify with any religion. "It seems that religion holds little sway over your spiritual practices." 5 Barna Research Group

The questions at hand in perspective of these findings are <u>how can you reject Jesus Christ and the word of God and expect to live your life in God's will, and what about heaven and eternity</u>?

5 Barna Research Group, *Faith and Christianity*, April 16, 2017

"The kingdom of heaven is like unto a certain king, which made a marriage for his son, And sent forth his servants to call them that were bidden to the wedding: and they would not come." (Mat. 22:2-3) What other way can you get to heaven if you don't heed God's invitation?

The world can be categorized in three ways:

1. Selfish gain – what's in it for me attitude; that's all that matters
2. Thoughtless waste – taking the goodness of God for granted
3. Endless frustration – those who live and die on their own terms

"And because iniquity shall abound, the love of many shall wax cold."(Mat. 24:12)

Are we living in a changing world, or has the attitude of indifference always existed? Has the emphasis on man become more important than the emphasis on God?

The invitation from God stands for mankind. He provided his way, even unto the sacrifice of his Son on the cross to bring you to him. "Again, he sent forth other servants, saying, Tell them which are bidden, Behold, I have prepared my dinner: my oxen and my fatlings are killed, and all things are ready: come unto the marriage. But they made light of it, and went their ways, one to his farm, another to his merchandise: And the remnant took his servants, and entreated them spitefully, and slew them." (Mat. 22:4-6)

Israel rejected Jesus Christ as their Messiah. "He came unto his own, and his own received him not." (John 1:11) But the whole world today seems to have issues with accepting the truth. Belief in God is not the same as accepting his Son as the savior of the world. "...the devils also believe, and tremble." (Jam. 2:19)

Self- Gain

The selfish attitude is just that, a self-centered perspective on life. Obviously, the free feast was not enough to entice these invited guests. If this represents Israel, all should see that God is offended with this blatant rejection. What about all the others that believe in God but have no time for him? Could there be more gain than spending all of eternity with a loving God? Rejecting this invitation is nothing more than a selfish act of indifference.

Communities today have changed because of big business taking over. All over America you can see remnants of main streets because big store chains have built these mega stores and malls that left some looking like ghost towns. The insult to injury is when these struggling stores have to go out of business and discount merchandise 50-75% off. Then the community shows up, not to support them, but to swoop down like vultures and finish them off and clean them out.

The church has this type of behavior when you can get more people to come out for a pot-luck dinner than for regular services to hear a life-changing gospel. Some have turned this into "pigeon religion." You throw down food, they swoop down, then they're gone again.

Taking Things for Granted

If we go down the road to see how much we can benefit or gain, are we missing the most important things in life? You can't treat the Christian life recklessly and expect full benefit from the Lord. Things that are present today were not always free in society. It took faithful men and women to fight the good fight to make sure we have the freedom to worship and practice our Christian beliefs.

A child of a very intelligent couple grew up making excellent grades in school and went to college and aced all his classes. He fell in with a few individuals who had to take drugs to stay up long hours to study. One day, he decided to try these out and found out that he could enjoy the high and keep his grades up. He stayed up for two days before the final exam and went in to take the test, when his heart collapsed and he died immediately.

Taking for granted the situation and never being thankful or grateful enough to pass along God's blessings to someone else is considered selfish and sinful. "Whereas ye know not what shall be on the morrow. For what is your life? It is even a vapour, that appeareth for a little time, and then vanisheth away. For that ye ought to say, If the Lord will, we shall live, and do this, or that. But now ye rejoice in your boastings: all such rejoicing is evil. Therefore to him that knoweth to do good, and doeth it not, to him it is sin." (Jam. 4:14-17)

The Most High

In Daniel's day, the King of all Babylon and territories beyond witnessed a miracle when three Hebrew men wouldn't bow down to a golden image he had made representing himself. "Then Nebuchadnezzar came near to the mouth of the burning fiery furnace, and spake, and said, Shadrach, Meshach, and Abednego, ye servants of the most high God, come forth, and come hither. Then Shadrach, Meshach, and Abednego, came forth of the midst of the fire. And the princes, governors, and captains, and the king's counsellors, being gathered together, saw these men, upon whose bodies the fire had no power, nor was an hair on their head singed, neither were their coats changed, nor the smell of fire had passed on them. Then Nebuchadnezzar spake, and said, Blessed be the God of Shadrach, Meshach, and Abednego, who hath sent his angel, and delivered his servants that trusted in him, and have changed the king's word, and yielded their bodies, that they might not serve nor worship any god, except their own God. Therefore I make a decree, That every people, nation, and language, which speak anything amiss against the God of Shadrach, Meshach, and Abednego, shall be cut in pieces, and their houses shall be made a dunghill: because there is no other God who can deliver after this sort." (Dan. 3:26-29)

The question is at this point, did King Nebuchadnezzar believe this in his heart? Could he make a decree and intend on not practicing what he so stately announced himself? As we would say today, "practice what you preach," or become a hypocrite.

Taking a Stand

Nebuchadnezzar lived in a polytheistic world where he had a favorite god, but this wasn't the most high God. It is true that God knows the hearts of all people, and he knew this man would verbally speak of the high God, but what was the purpose? "I thought it good to shew the signs and wonders that the high God hath wrought toward me. How great are his signs! and how mighty are his wonders! his kingdom is an everlasting kingdom, and his dominion is from generation to generation." (Dan. 4:2-3) Let everyone know how great I am and how God has blessed me. The Bible tells us about this sort of thing. "Wherefore let him that thinketh he standeth take heed lest he fall." (I Cor. 10:12)

Only God can put people to the real test. This man is the most powerful man alive in this day, but there is one whom he still needs to answer to. Could it be that this king made "light of it," indifferent?

"I Nebuchadnezzar was at rest in mine house, and flourishing in my palace: I saw a dream which made me afraid, and the thoughts upon my bed and the visions of my head troubled me. Therefore I made a decree to bring in all the wise men of Babylon before me, that they might make known unto me the interpretation of the dream. (Dan. 4:4-6)

He called all the magicians, the soothsayers, astrologers, and none knew the interpretation of the frightening incident. Call in the man with the God on his side. "But at the last Daniel came in before me, whose name was Belteshazzar, according to the name of my god, and in whom is the spirit of the holy gods: and before him I told the dream, saying, O Belteshazzar master of the magicians, because I know that the spirit of the holy gods is in thee, and no secret troubleth thee, tell me the visions of my dream that I have seen, and the interpretation thereof." (Dan. 4:8-9) When all else fails don't we have the tendency to then pray and go to the Pastor with our troubles?

This man Belteshazzar, Daniel, must have been his favorite to have named him after his god. Why send all the pompous spiritualists in first? Could it be that the King didn't really want to accept this truth of his dreams and visions? The thought of putting off the inevitable all the while thinking that things might change or go away is delusional. The Christian tries this continuously, but God has placed that still, small voice of the Holy Spirit inside to guide us to his will, yet is going neglected too often.

As the Pharaoh of Egypt in Moses' day, the message was to "let my people go," as God dealt with that stubborn pagan leader. The message directed toward this king is a very personal one to "let other gods go," and worship the one and only most high God. After all, he did make a decree for everyone else.

The Dream

"Thus were the visions of mine head in my bed; I saw, and behold a tree in the midst of the earth, and the height thereof was great. The tree grew, and was strong, and the height thereof reached unto heaven, and the sight thereof to the end of all the earth: The leaves thereof were fair, and the fruit thereof much, and it was meat for all: the beasts of the field had shadow under it, and the fowls of the heaven dwelt in the boughs thereof, and all flesh was fed of it. I saw in the visions of my head upon my bed, and, behold, a watcher and an holy one came down from heaven; He cried aloud, and said thus, Hew down the tree, and cut off his branches, shake off his leaves, and scatter his fruit: let the beasts get away from under it, and the fowls from his branches: Nevertheless leave the stump of his roots in the earth, even with a band of iron and brass, in the tender grass of the field; and let it be wet with the dew of heaven, and let his portion be with the beasts in the grass of the earth: Let his heart be changed from man's, and let a beast's heart be given unto him; and let seven times pass over him. This matter is by the decree of the watchers, and the demand by the word of the holy ones: to the intent that the living may know that the most

High ruleth in the kingdom of men, and giveth it to whomsoever he will, and setteh up over it the basest of men." (Dan. 4:10-17)

A Lesson in Humility

Bad news is hard to break to anyone, but necessary. Daniel was reluctant to break this prophetic interpretation to the King, but the King pressed him. If only we could know the future, or even twelve months of time, we would try to change things to make them better. But this fate had been declared from heavenly angels, relaying the message from the Most High God.

"At the end of twelve months he walked in the palace of the kingdom of Babylon. The king spake, and said, Is not this great Babylon, that I have built for the house of the kingdom by the might of my power, and the honour of my majesty?" (Dan. 4:29-30) How long does it take to sink in after Daniel had interpreted the vision to him that he indeed, and his kingdom, will fall for seven years? "Pride goeth before destruction, and an haughty spirit before a fall." (Prov. 16:18)

"While the word was in the king's mouth, there fell a voice from heaven, saying, O king Nebuchadnezzar, to thee it is spoken; The kingdom is departed from thee." (Dan. 4:31) Notice the angel didn't say, "thy kingdom," is departed from thee. Saying that this great majesty that you so proudly claim is none other than God's kingdom, but he allowed you to run it. But, now you must learn a lesson in humility.

In the day of Noah, the people did not believe the world would flood, in fact they made light of it. The sin of indifference is not as much unbelief but a "don't care" attitude, stemming from a self-sufficient heart. Some think their life, career, family, etc. is more superior, better than anyone else's. No gratefulness to God and his rich blessings and day to day watchful care.

Pride will lift you up as James 4:6 states, "But he giveth more grace. Wherefore he saith, God resisteth the proud, but giveth grace unto the humble." Agnostics don't care if there is a God or anything beyond this physical world. Does this state of mind change any spiritual facts? To ignore sin is foolish and dangerous. "The fool hath said in his heart, There is no God. They are corrupt, they have done abominable works, there is none that doeth good." (Psa. 14:1)

Reconciled and Restored

"The same hour was the thing fulfilled upon Nebuchadnezzar: and he was driven from men, and did eat grass as oxen, and his body was wet with the dew of heaven, till his hairs were grown like eagles' feathers, and his nails like birds' claws." (Dan. 4:33) One can only speculate how God dealt with this man internally during his seven years of judgment, but I would mention that he surely had some understanding in himself to absorb this most valuable lesson. "The sacrifices of God are a broken spirit: a broken and a contrite heart, O God, thou wilt not despise." (Psa. 51:17)

"And at the end of the days I Nebuchadnezzar lifted up mine eyes unto heaven, and mine understanding returned unto me, and I blessed the most High, and I praised and honoured him that liveth for ever, whose dominion is an everlasting dominion, and his kingdom is from generation to generation." (Dan. 4:34) "At the same time my reason returned unto me; and for the glory of my kingdom, mine honour and brightness returned unto me; and my counsellors and my lords sought unto me; and I was established in my kingdom, and excellent majesty was added unto me. Now I Nebuchadnezzar praise and extol and honour the King of heaven, all whose works are truth, and his ways judgment: and those that walk in pride he is able to abase." (Dan. 4:36-37)

A Christian can bring themselves into a frustrating position by not letting God be God. The saying that "If the Lord is not Lord of all, he is not Lord at all," carries a lot of truth. The Lord offers <u>understanding</u> and <u>reasoning,</u> but how much of these we allow him to give depends on our yielding.

"The Christian way is different: harder, and easier. Christ says, 'Give me All. I don't want so much of your time and so much of your money and so much of your work: I want you. I have not come to torment your natural self, but to kill it'. No half measures are any good." 6 (C.S. Lewis)

Higher Thinking

Anxiety, trouble, and despair should be converted to peace, harmony, and joy. Consider taking the high road with a better relationship with the Lord by:

1. Refusing to lean on your own understanding – (Proverbs 3:5-6)

2. Accepting his wisdom and reasoning – (I Corinthians 3:18-20)

Many Christians complain of not growing spiritually, but people have a tendency to leave their life in a cruise mode, a niche, a schedule, that feels timely and comfortable to them.

The problem that is happening with this mentality is that the Holy Spirit keeps trying to get their attention, nudge them, knock on their heart's door, and they are in a self-locked position. They are necessarily conformed to this world, as Romans 12:2 suggests, but they are conformed to their own selves. You can't be your own entity. "I am the vine, ye are the branches. He that abideth in me, and I in him, the same bringeth forth much fruit: for without me ye can do nothing." (John 15:5)

---

6 C.S. Lewis, *Mere Christianity*, Harper Collins Publisher 1952, pg. 196

BIBLIOGRAPHY

Bob Jones, "Do Right," The Sword of the Lord Publishers, Murfreesboro TN, 1971

William P. Barker, *Everyone in the Bible*, Fleming H. Revell Co. Westwood, NJ

Charles F, Stanley, *Confronting Casual Christianity*, Broadman Press, 1985

Oliver B. Greene, "Why Does the Devil Desire to Damn You?" The Gospel Hour, 1966

Barna Research Group, *Faith and Christianity*, April 16, 2017

C.S. Lewis, *Mere Christianity*, Harper Collins Publisher 1952

Study Guide

Church Resource for Classroom and Personal Study

Take the High Road
Doing the Right thing

Are Christians Accountable for Their Actions?

Section I

- ❖ The Consequences of Sin
- ❖ God at Work
- ❖ God's Divine Ways
- ❖ Rich Toward God

I. Christians are saved, but what about the consequences of sin?

A. The influences of Christianity are made void when one sins because actions speak louder than words. Sin has no power over you.

- I Corinthians 6:9-12, "Know ye not that the unrighteous shall not inherit the kingdom of God? Be not deceived: neither fornicators, nor idolaters, nor adulterers, nor effeminate, nor abusers of themselves with mankind, nor thieves, nor covetous, nor drunkards, nor revilers, nor extortioners, shall inherit the kingdom of God. And such were some of you: but ye are washed, but ye are sanctified, but ye are justified in the name of the Lord Jesus, and by the

Spirit of our God. All things are lawful unto me, but all things are not expedient: all things are lawful for me, but I will not be brought under the power of any."

B. We can only bring shame upon God by bad lasting impressions.
- Romans 14:7-8, "<u>For none of us liveth to himself</u>, and <u>no man dieth to himself</u>. For whether we live, we live unto the Lord; and whether we die, we die unto the Lord: whether we live therefore, or we die, we are the Lord's."

C. People outside the Church need someone right with God.
- I Peter 2:12, "<u>Having your conversation honest</u> among the Gentiles: that, whereas they <u>speak against you as evildoers</u>, <u>they may by your good works</u>, <u>which they shall behold</u>, <u>glorify God</u> in the day of visitation."

    1. Your family needs an anchor for assurance of their right relationship to God. They know you well.

- Matthew 13:57, "A prophet is not <u>without honour</u>, save in his own country, <u>and in his own house</u>."

    2. Why should your family take God seriously if you don't?

- I Corinthians 8:9, "But take heed lest by any means <u>this liberty of yours become a stumblingblock</u> to them that are weak."

D. Does God measure my love for others?

- I John 3:17, "But whoso hath this world's good, and <u>seeth</u> <u>his brother have need</u>, and <u>shutteth up</u>

his bowels of <u>compassion</u> from him, <u>how dwelleth the love of God</u> in him?"

E. A deeper commitment, not superficial, but sacrificial. Flesh or Spirit?

- I John 4:17, "Herein is our love made perfect, that we may have boldness in the day of judgment: <u>because as he is</u>, <u>so</u> <u>are we in this world</u>."

F. When our attitude is right with God, right actions will follow.

- I Timothy 6:6, "But godliness with contentment is great gain."

II. God at Work.

Consider the many ways you can observe God working:

A. Hands for charity.

- Deuteronomy 15:7-8, "If there be among you a poor man... <u>thou shalt not harden thine heart, nor shut thine hand</u>... thou shalt open thine hand wide unto him, and shalt surely lend him sufficient for his need..." (see Jam. 2:15-16)

B. Eyes to see his power.

- II Kings 6:16-17, (Syrian army attack), "Fear not: for they that be with us are more than they that be with them. And Elisha prayed, and said, Lord, I pray thee, open his eyes, that he may see." <u>Spiritual power is real</u>.

C. Ears to hear him.

- Proverbs 15:31, "The ear that heareth the reproof of life abideth among the wise." <u>The wise listens</u> (see Mat. 11:15)

D. Lips for your testimony.

- Psalms 107:2, "Let the redeemed of the Lord say so, whom he hath redeemed from the hand of the enemy." <u>Christians rejoice</u>.

E. Make a stand for prayer.

- Daniel 6:10, "Now when Daniel knew that the writing was signed, he went into his house; and his windows being open... kneeled upon his knees three times a day, and prayed..." <u>Godly courage</u>.

F. Be receptive to God's message.

- I Peter 2:2, "As newborn babes, desire the sincere milk of the word, that ye may grow thereby.

" <u>Spiritual growth</u> (see Mat. 13:23)

G. Desire good works.

- I Corinthians 3:9, "For we are labourers together with God: ye are God's husbandry, ye are God's building."

God is working with others, he wants you to walk with him also.

<u>1</u>. the Christian life is public for everyone to see; your message will be positive or negative

2. God sees more of your works, fleshly or spiritually motivated

3. the judge will one day try by fire what sort your works are; "Every man's work shall be made manifest: for the day shall declare it, because it shall be revealed by fire; and the fire shall try every man's work of what sort it is." (I Cor. 3:13)

III. God's Divine Ways.

God's Ways are higher than man's.

Isaiah 55:9, "For as the heavens are higher than the earth, so are my ways higher than your ways, and my thoughts than your thoughts."

A. The Spirit of God reveals God's thoughts.

- I Corinthians 2:12, "Now we have <u>received</u>, not the <u>spirit</u> of the <u>world</u>, but the <u>spirit which is of God</u>; that we might <u>know</u> <u>the things that are freely given to us of God</u>." Verse 16; "...we have the mind of Christ."

B. Man's natural thoughts are not God's.

- I Corinthians 2:14, "But the natural man <u>receiveth not</u> the things of the Spirit of God: for

they are <u>foolishness unto him</u>: neither can he know them, because they are <u>spiritually discerned</u>." Verse 11; "For what man knoweth the things of a man, save the <u>spirit of man which is in him</u>?"
1. Man is born with natural thoughts and learns the world's ways until he is indoctrinated
2. God's thoughts are not a part of his life until Salvation
3. The Holy Spirit will guide the new believer while the flesh struggles

C. The search for happiness is the main thrust for society, as Solomon states:
- Ecclesiastes 2;10, "And whatsoever mine eyes desired I kept not from them, I withheld not my heart from any joy; for my heart rejoiced in all my labour: and this was my portion of all my labour."
1. The flesh knows no limit to reach for happiness
2. The flesh is insatiable and never stops trying to fulfill

D. Was Solomon entitled to the fruits of his labor?

- Ecclesiastes 2:11, "<u>Then I looked on all the works</u> that my hands had wrought, and on the labour that I had laboured to do: and, behold, all was <u>vanity and vexation of spirit</u>, and there was <u>no profit</u> under the sun."

E. The temporary satisfaction of fulfilling the flesh wears off. How much alcohol, drugs, even food is enough to give you satisfaction?

- Ephesians 5:18, "And be not drunk with wine, wherein is excess; but be filled with the Spirit."

F. God shall provide you joy for your labors.

- Ecclesiastes 5:18-20, "Behold that which I have seen: it is good and comely for one to eat and to drink, and to enjoy the good of all his labour that he taketh under the sun all the days of his life, which God giveth him: for it is his portion. Every man also to whom God hath given riches and wealth, and hath given him power to eat thereof, and to take his portion, and to rejoice in his labour; this is the gift of God. For he shall not much remember the days of his life; because God answereth him in the joy of his heart."

IV. Rich Toward God.
Is having Wealth Sin?

A. Seeking fame and fortune, and focusing entirely on riches is self-pride and arrogance in the eyes of the Lord. e.g. the rich man who needed bigger barns to hold all his goods:

- Luke 12:17-21, "And he thought within himself, saying, What shall I do, because I have no room where to bestow my fruits? And he said, This will I do: I will pull down my barns, and build greater; and there will I bestow all my fruits and my goods. And I will say to my soul, Soul, thou hast much goods laid up for many years; take thine ease, eat, drink, and be merry. But God said unto him, Thou fool, this night thy soul shall be required of thee: then whose shall those things be, which thou hast provided? So is he that layeth up treasure for himself, and is not rich toward God."

B. Solomon had lavish wealth:
1. the temple had golden mortar
2. 700 wives, 300 concubines
3. 40,000 horses and chariots
4. 12,000 horsemen
    ➢ He concluded, all was vanity and vexation of spirit.

- Proverbs 13:7-8, "There is that maketh himself rich, yet <u>hath nothing</u>: there is that maketh himself <u>poor</u>, yet hath <u>great riches</u>. The <u>ransom of a man's life are his riches</u>: but the poor heareth <u>not rebuke</u>." (answering to others because of money)

C. Life is made up of more than riches, but spiritual satisfaction. A life separated from God and a life separated to God are quite different. We are his workmanship.

- Ephesians 2:10, "For we are his <u>workmanship, created in</u> Christ Jesus unto good works, which God hath <u>before</u> <u>ordained</u> that we should walk in them."

D. The life away from God is a futile experience.
    Consider the characteristics:
    1. Life is utterly futile – what's the use in trying
    2. Repetitive – same old thing everyday
    3. Sorrowful – no happiness, no joy, no good
    4. Grievous and frustrating – getting nowhere
    5. Uncertain – no peace

6. Without purpose – what's the use, no goals
7. Incurable – basket case
8. Unjust – will cheat to get ahead
9. Mere existence – surviving day to day, not living

- Proverbs 1:24, "Because I have <u>called</u>, and <u>ye refused</u>; I have <u>stretched out my hand</u>, and <u>no man regarded</u>."

E. God's plan is the higher road than men can obtain through Jesus Christ.
   1. Plants have one sense – a sense of existence
   2. Animals have two senses – existence and self-awareness
   3. Mankind has three senses – existence, self-awareness, and God awareness

- Matthew 6:26, "Behold the fowls of the air: for they sow not, neither do they reap, nor gather into barns; yet your heavenly Father feedeth them. <u>Are ye not much better</u> than they?"

➢ We all make choices and decisions each day of our lives. Making these important and life-changing actions will determine how we end up in life.

TEST YOUR KNOWLEDGE
SECTION I

1. Does sin affect people around you? Yes _____ No _____

2. Complete these verses found in Romans 14:7-8 – "For none of us _____ to himself, and no man _____ to himself. For whether we _____, we live unto the _____; and whether we die, we die unto the _____: whether we live therefore, or die, we are the Lord's."

3. Jesus said in Matthew 13:57, "A prophet is not without honour, save in his own country, and his own house." According to this application, who knows you best if you are a committed Christian? (check all that apply)

    a. your family ___

    b. your workplace ___

    c. your city ___

    d. your country ___

4. If you don't take God seriously, does your family take you seriously? Yes _____ No _____

5. Select the ways you can see God working in people's lives (check all that apply)

    Hands for charity _____

    Eyes to see his power _____

    Lips for testimony _____

    Working for riches _____

    Not reading your Bible _____

6. The Christian's life is for everyone to see. True ___ False ___

7. Complete this verse found in I Corinthians 3:13 – "Every man's work shall be made _____: for the day shall _____ it, because it shall be _____ by fire; and the _____ shall try every man's work of what _____ it is."

8. God's ways are higher than our ways. In what verse can this truth be found? _____

9. God's thoughts are not a part of a person until the moment of S _ _ _ _ _ _ _ _.

10. "But the natural man receiveth not the things of the Spirit of God: because they are _____ unto him."

   a. not true ___

   b. foolishness ___

   c. unwise ___

11. Who said, "Then I looked on all the works that my hands had wrought, and on the labour that I had laboured to do: and, behold, all was vanity and vexation of spirit, and there was no profit under the sun." and where is it found? _____, _____

12. The flesh will never be satisfied without the Holy Spirit. True ___ False ___

13. The rich man of Jesus' parable in Luke 12:17-21 was judged by God with what quote? "Thou _____, this _____ _____ _____ _____ ___ _____ ____ _____."

14. Complete this verse found in Proverbs 13:8 – "The _____ of a man's life are his _____: but the poor heareth not _____."

15. God's plan is higher and can be obtained through – J_____ C_____

Take the High Road
Doing the Right Thing

Trying to Do the Right Thing Goes Nowhere Without God.

Section II

- ❖ **Taking Matters into Your Own Hands**
- ❖ **Grace Abounds**
- ❖ **Judge Me Not**

I. Taking Matters Into Your Own Hands.

A. The right thing can backfire: Moses killed the Egyptian taskmaster.

- Exodus 2:13-15, "And when he went out the second day, behold, two men of the Hebrews strove together: and he said to him that did the wrong, Wherefore smitest thou thy fellow? And he said, <u>Who made thee a prince and a judge over us</u>? <u>intendest thou to kill me</u>, <u>as thou killedst the Egyptian</u>? And Moses feared, and said, Surely this thing is known. Now when Pharaoh heard this thing, <u>he sought to slay Moses</u>. But Moses fled from the face of Pharaoh, and dwelt in the <u>land of Midian</u>: and he sat down by a well."
  1. he tried to protect his brethren
  2. he fled because of the backlash and blame

B. Moses made a life-changing decision motivated by character and faith.

- Hebrews 11:24-26, "<u>By faith Moses</u>, when he was come to years, <u>refused to be called the son of Pharaoh's daughter</u>; Choosing rather to <u>suffer affliction</u> with the people of God, than to enjoy the pleasures of sin for a season. Esteeming the <u>reproach of Christ greater riches than the treasures in Egypt</u>: for he had respect unto the recompense of the reward."
  1. Moses chose identification with God over the Egyptians
  2. he has stepped out in faith

C. This is God's plan and purpose for Moses.

- Romans 9:17, "For the scripture saith unto Pharaoh, Even for this <u>same purpose have I raised thee up</u>, that <u>I might</u> <u>shew my power in thee</u>, and <u>that my name might be declared</u> <u>throughout all the earth</u>."
  1. does God care for the Israelites?
  2. 400 years of slavery, now the exodus is at hand
     a. God's terms
     b. God's man
     c. God's timing
- Luke 1:50, "And his mercy is on them that fear him from generation to generation."

D. Taking the high road is not easy; sin will need to be dealt with:

1. Moses' sin was exposed - Ex. 2:14

2. the Holy Spirit will show you your sins – Num. 32:23

E. Your self-independence, self-rule, and self-pride is an issue.

- James 4:13-17, "Go to now, <u>ye that say</u>, To day or to morrow we will go into such a city, and continue there a year, and buy and sell, and get gain: <u>whereas ye know not what shall be on the morrow. For what is your life?</u> It is even a <u>vapour</u>, that appeareth for a little time, and then <u>vanisheth away</u>. For that ye ought to say, <u>If the Lord will</u>, <u>we shall live</u>, <u>and do this, or that</u>. But now ye rejoice in your boastings: all such rejoicing is evil. Therefore to him <u>that knoweth to do good</u>, <u>and doeth it not, to him it is sin</u>."
  1. don't pray for God to bless your decisions, pray for him to lead you to the right decision
  2. your life can get out of control
  3. never too late to do over
  4. wait for God to answer

II. Grace Abounds
God knows the believer and sees his sin that so easily besets him or her.

- A. He has omnipotence over death and life, omniscience over all the earth, and he is omnipresent in your life.

- Ephesians 4:7-10, "But unto every one of us is given grace according to the measure of the gift of Christ. Wherefore he saith, When he ascended up on high, he led captivity captive, and gave gifts unto men. (Now that he ascended, what is it but that he also descended first into the lower parts of the earth? He that descended is the same also that ascended up far above all heavens, that he might fill all things.)"
  1. he has captured what has captured you
  2. victory belongs to Jesus

3. his grace he gives to you

B. Grace will bring peace when we direct our lives toward God.

- Romans 8:28 "And we know that all things work together for good to them that love God, to them who are the called according to his purpose."
  1. suppression leads to: stagnation – no life
  2. yielding leads to: right living, right decisions, success in life

C. "It is my way or I will not do it at all," is the main standard today. Free speech, free sexuality, free religion; the behavior of human souls as Cain, the first child.

- Genesis 4:3-5, "And in the process of time it came to pass, that Cain brought of the fruit of the ground an offering unto the Lord. And Abel, he also brought of the firstlings of his flock and of the fat thereof. And the Lord had respect unto Abel and to his offering: But unto Cain and to his offering he had not respect. And Cain was very wroth, and his countenance fell." (Abel's offering of blood, Cain of the ground)
  1. Why did Cain get upset over God's reply?
  2. "you will have to accept me as I am" attitude

• Genesis 4:6-8, "And the Lord said unto Cain, Why art thou wroth? and why is thy countenance fallen? If thou doest well, shalt thou not be accepted? And if thou doest not well, sin lieth at the door. And unto thee shalt be his desire, and thou shalt rule over him. And Cain talked with Abel his brother: and it came to pass when they were in the field, that Cain rose up against Abel his brother, and slew him."

D. Who is the authority after all? It is God's way or sin will have its way.
   1. the second chance from God to Cain proves God's grace
   2. Cain so vehemently believed in his stand to murder Abel

E. God warns the believer through the Holy Spirit of this clear danger of sin.

- Luke 12:5; "But I will forewarn you whom shall ye fear: Fear him, which after he hath killed hath power to cast into hell; yea, I say unto you, Fear him."
   1. take this warning seriously
   2. this is not a preference as everything else is today
   3. sin will be judged

III. Judge Me Not.
People Will Not Accept the Fact of Judgment.

A. What kind of life can you live with the weight of sin, guilt, shame. Pride, etc.?

- Hebrews 9:27," It is appointed unto men once to die, but after this the judgment."

B. Poor and unwise choices are like driving your car into a ditch.

- Proverbs 30:24, "There be four things which are little upon the earth, but they are exceeding wise." This verse is referring to the ants, conies (rabbits), locusts, and spiders.
   1. these can foresee their future
   2. are people wiser than one of these

C. God's high road versus man's low road that leads to:
   1. dangerous risks
   2. constant struggle
   3. continuous trouble
   4. no peace
      ➢ Sin is like a leopard ready to pounce "at the door" with consequences.

D. Consider the Asian plant Kudzu, used for soil erosion.
   1. introduced in the U.S. in the late 1800's
   2. 85 million seedlings distributed
   3. by 1946, 3 million acres planted
   4. became totally invasive, engulfing whole trees
   5. killing anything that gets in its way
   6. considered in 1970 to be a noxious weed and a dangerous vine

E. The wisdom of God knows the Christian's temptations.

   James 1:14-16, "But every man is tempted, when he is drawn away of his own lust and enticed. Then when lust hath conceived, it bringeth forth sin: and sin, when it is finished, bringeth forth death. Do not err, my beloved brethren."
   1. we can get entangled in temptations
   2. only through the Lord, can we find a clear path again

F. Letting God help you break free by taking these required steps:
   1. Accept Christ as Savior – "Therefore if any man be in Christ, he is a new creature: old things are passed away; behold, all things are become new." II Cor. 5:17

2. Let God start working – "Submit yourselves therefore to God, Resist the devil and he will flee from you." Jam. 4:7
3. Mortify the flesh – "Knowing this, that our old man is crucified with him, that the body of sin might be destroyed, that henceforth we should not serve sin." Rom.6:6
4. Reading the Word of God – "Thy word is a lamp unto my feet, and a light unto my path." Psa. 119:105
5. Gain knowledge and wisdom – "The fear of the Lord is the beginning of knowledge: but fools despise wisdom and instruction." Prov. 1:7
6. Join a Bible believing Church – "Not forsaking the assembling of ourselves together, as the manner of some is; but exhorting one another; and so much the more, as ye see the day approaching." Heb. 10:25
7. Yielding to the Holy Spirit – "I beseech you therefore, brethren, by the mercies of God, that ye present your bodies a living sacrifice, holy, acceptable unto God, which is your reasonable service. And be not conformed to this world: but be ye transformed by the renewing of your mind, that ye may prove what is that good, and acceptable, and perfect, will of God." Rom. 12:1-2

TEST YOUR KNOWLEDGE

SECTION II

1. What made Moses flee from Egypt?
    a. he wanted to live as a Hebrew ___
    b. he couldn't tolerate slavery ___
    c. he killed a man ___
2. After 400 years of slavery, God would deliver his people out of Egypt. What three components worked together for this to happen?
    a. God's _____
    b. God's _____
    c. God's _____
3. Taking the high road is not easy; sin will have to be dealt with. True ___ False ___
4. Complete this verse found in James 4:17 – "Therefore to him that _____ to do good, and _____ ___ ___, to him it is _____."
5. Grace will bring peace when we direct our lives toward God. Suppression leads to_____
Yielding leads to_____
6. Cain slew his brother Abel because he was jealous of his approval from God. Could Cain have received approval from God? Yes ___ No ___, if so, what kind of offering would be sufficient? _____
7. Did God prove that he gives grace by giving Cain a second chance? Yes ___ No ___
8. Complete this verse found in Genesis 4:7 – "If thou doest _____, shalt thou not be _____? and if thou doest _____, ___ lieth at the door. And unto thee shall be his _____, and thou shalt rule over him."
9. Judgment is inevitable for all, and the appointment for

your death is already made in heaven. True ___ False ___

10. Complete this verse found in Hebrews 9:27 – "It is _____ unto men _____ to ____, but after this the _____."

11. Temptations will lead to sin if the believer is not wise. List the four step danger found in James 1:14-16:
   a. T _____
   b. L _____
   c. S _____
   d. D _____

12. What are the required steps that will let God's grace help you?
   a. Accept _____ as _____ - verse _____
   b. Let God _____ _____ - verse _____
   c. Mortify the _____ - verse _____
   d. Read the _____ of _____ - verse _____
   e. Gain _____ and _____ - verse _____
   f. Join a _____ _____ Church – verse _____
   g. Yield to the _____ _____ - verses _____

Take the High Road
Doing the Right Thing

You are Considered Valuable to Heaven

Section III

- ❖ The Temporal and the Eternal
- ❖ Who's In Control
- ❖ Light Shines in a Dark Place

I. There is too much emphasis on the temporal and not enough on the eternal.

A. The world was blind to who Jesus was and what he brought to this world.

- John 1:5, "And the light shineth in darkness; and the darkness <u>comprehended it not</u>."

B. The forerunner of Jesus came to this world understanding the light from heaven.

- John 1:6-8, "There was a <u>man sent from God,</u> whose name was <u>John</u>. The same came for a <u>witness</u>, to bear witness of the <u>Light</u>, that all men through him <u>might believe</u>. He was not that Light, but was sent to bear witness of that Light."

C. When a person accepts Christ, the change from earthly thinking to a new righteousness from God transpires.
  1. you are no longer dependent on the world's ways
  2. you have eternal thoughts
  3. God has a plan for you
  4. the world misunderstands you
  5. you can become a threat by your spirituality

- Matthew 6:28-29, "And why take ye thought for rainment? Consider the lilies of the field, how they grow; they toil not, neither do they spin: And yet I say unto you, That even Solomon in all his glory was not arrayed like one of these."

D. The Christian is anointed to live here to bear witness of the truth, which is different and difficult for the world to accept.

- John 17:14-18, "I have given them thy word; and the world hath hated them, because they are not of the world, even as I am not of the world. I pray not that thou shouldest take them out of the world, but that thou shouldest keep them from the evil. They are not of the world, even as I am not of the world. Sanctify them through thy truth: thy word is truth. As thou hast sent me into the world, even so have I also sent them into the world."

E. John the Baptist dared to live as a witness.

  1. separate from the sins of the people
  2. he offered the message of repentance

II. Who's in control?
Your old life carries sinful habits.

A. There are lusts attached to your life you can't depart with.

- Romans 6:12, "Let not sin therefore <u>reign</u> in your mortal body, that ye <u>should obey</u> it in the lusts thereof."

B. Why does a person have to clean up his life because he accepts Christ? Can we?
  1. we can't do it ourselves, the Holy Spirit guides us
  2. from a lump of coal to a diamond in the rough

- John 14:26, "But the Comforter, which is the <u>Holy Ghost</u>, whom the Father will send in my name, he shall <u>teach you all things</u>, and bring all things to <u>your remembrance</u>, whatsoever I said unto you."

C. How valuable you are to the world depends on your following their agenda.
  1. starts with an ungodly agenda – politics, theater, music, art, etc. (II Tim. 2:4)
  2. fueled by Satan's ambitions – his plan must progress, time is short (Rev. 12:12)
  3. humans are disposable – war, talent, worth, etc. (ex. Tower of Babel)
  4. ever-enduring cycle – keep up or get left behind as not valuable

- John 16:33, "...In the world ye shall have tribulation: but be of good cheer; I have <u>overcome the world</u>."

D. The Christian stands between God and the devil in this world, facing a constant struggle.

- I John 2:20-22, "But ye have an <u>unction from the Holy One</u>, and <u>ye know all things</u>. I have not written unto you because ye know not the truth, but because ye know it, and that no lie is of the truth. Who is a <u>liar</u> but he that <u>denieth</u> that Jesus is the Christ? He is <u>antichrist</u>, that denieth the Father and the Son."

- I John 5:18-19, "We know that whosoever is <u>born of God sinneth not</u>; but he that is begotten of God keepeth himself, and that <u>wicked one toucheth him not</u>. And we know that we are of God, and the <u>whole world lieth in wickedness</u>."

- Matthew 12:33, "Either make the <u>tree good</u>, and his <u>fruit good</u>; or else make the tree <u>corrupt</u>, and his <u>fruit corrupt</u>: for the tree is <u>known by his fruit</u>."

E. The world has good in it, because the Holy Spirit is holding back evil until the rapture.
   - II Thessalonians 2:7, "For the mystery of iniquity doth already work: only <u>he who now letteth will let</u>, <u>until he be taken out of the way</u>."

III. Light shines in a darkened place.

Let your light shine for the world to see.

A. Your light comes by the Holy Spirit entering into your life and changing you to a new hope and purpose of life.

- Matthew 5:16, "Let your <u>light so shine before men</u>, that they may <u>see your good works</u>, and <u>glorify your Father</u> which is in heaven."
    1. it is a tragedy that the light is barely seen in some
    2. some are being oppressed or misguided by circumstance

B. Isaiah's situation in life left him discouraged to know sin and wickedness ruled the earth. Was God the ruler over King Uzziah?

- Isaiah 6:1-3, "In the year that <u>King Uzziah died I saw also the Lord sitting upon a throne</u>, high and lifted up, and his train filled the temple. Above it stood the seraphims: each one had six wings; with twain he covered his face, and with twain he covered his feet, and with twain he did fly. And one cried unto another, and said, <u>Holy, holy, holy</u>, is the Lord of hosts: <u>the whole earth is full of his glory</u>."

    1. Why didn't Isaiah see all this before? Could he have been focusing on the wrong king? (earthly)
    2. Was the whole earth full of the glory of God always or just when Isaiah had the vision?
    3. Was it because of the darkness of men's hearts the light was oppressed?

C. This vision astonished Isaiah to analyze his heart and failures. His praise and prayers were restored.

- Isaiah 6:5-7, "Then said I, <u>Woe is me</u>! <u>for I am undone</u>; because I am a man of <u>unclean lips</u>, and I dwell in the midst of a people of unclean lips: for <u>mine eyes have seen the King</u>, the Lord of hosts. Then flew one of the seraphims unto me, having a live coal in his hand, which he had taken with the tongs from off the altar: And he laid it upon my mouth, and said, Lo, <u>this hath touched thy lips</u>; and <u>thine iniquity is taken away, and thy sin purged</u>."

D. What keeps a person from serving and glorifying God?

We all need the light to shine in our hearts and minds as Isaiah in his heavenly vision heard from God.

- Isaiah 6:8-10, "Also I heard the voice of the Lord, saying, <u>Whom shall I send</u>, and <u>who will go for us</u>? Then said I, <u>Here am I</u>; <u>send me</u>. And he said, Go, and tell this people, <u>Hear ye indeed</u>, <u>but understand not</u>; <u>and see ye indeed</u>, <u>but perceive not</u>. Make the heart of this people fat, and make their ears heavy, and shut their eyes; lest they <u>see with their eyes, and hear with their ears, and understand with their heart, and convert, and be healed</u>."

E. According to John 1:5, "And the light <u>shineth in darkness</u>: and the darkness comprehended it not." Meaning the light of Christ shines upon all men but we don't understand it.

> **God saw his Son in this world as the Light**

> **they put him to death because of the blindness of their hearts**

> **God raised him to provide eternal life**

- Romans 10:6-9, "But the righteousness which is of faith speaketh on this wise, Say not in thine heart, Who shall ascend into heaven? (that is, to bring down Christ from above:) Or, Who shall descend into the deep? (that is, to bring up Christ again from the dead.) But what saith it? <u>The word is nigh thee, even in thy mouth, and in thy heart</u>: that is, the word of faith, which we preach; that if <u>thou shalt confess with thy mouth the Lord Jesus, and shalt believe in thine heart that God hath raised him from the dead, thou shalt be saved.</u>"

TEST YOUR KNOWLEDGE

SECTION III

1. Who was the man that came to bear witness of the light? _____

2. When a person accepts Christ, a new righteousness transpires. What did Jesus liken it to in Matthew 6:28? _____ of the _____.

3. Complete these verses found in John 17:16-17 – "They are ____ of this _____, even as I am ____ of this _____, sanctify them through thy _____: thy _____ is truth."

4. We can clean up our lives ourselves after salvation. True ___ False ___

5. The Holy Spirit is present to:
    a. teach us all things ___
    b. comfort ___
    c. bring to remembrance the word ___
    d. all the above ___

6. You are valuable to the world if you keep an ungodly agenda. True ___ False ___

7. Jesus overcame the world as he states in John 16:33; does this mean everything on the devil's agenda? Yes ___ No ___

8. Complete this verse found in I John 2:22 – "Who is a _____ but he that_____ that Jesus is the _____? He is _____, that _____ the Father and the Son."

9. The tree is known by his _____. (Mat. 12:33)

10. The Holy Spirit is present holding back evil until when? R_____

11. When did Isaiah see the vision from God according to Isaiah 6:1? _____

12. The glory of God appears to a person as a light that opens up the eyes to the truth. True ___ False ___

13. Isaiah cried that he was a man of unclean lips; then what happened next?
_____
_____

14. Israel had a heart condition. They hear but _____ not, they see but _____ not.
Who did God send to tell them of this sin? _____

15. The light shineth in darkness and the darkness comprehended it not according to John 1:5; who does this refer to? J_____ C_____

16. According to Romans 10:9, there are two consecutive things that you must do before you get saved:
    a. C_____ with thy _____ the Lord Jesus
    b. B_____ in thine _____ that
    c. God hath _____ him from the _____

Take the High Road
Doing the Right Thing

Intentions

Section IV

❖ **No Delays**
❖ **Today has Come**
❖ **Your New Walk**

I. Need not delay.

A. Promises are broken unintentionally and they don't mean much to God if not acted upon promptly. Jesus states this issue.

- Luke 9:59-62, "And he said unto another, Follow me. But he said, Lord, suffer me first to go and bury my father. Jesus said unto him, Let the dead bury their dead: but go thou and preach the kingdom of God. And another also said, Lord, I will follow thee; but let me first go bid them farewell, which are at home at my house. And Jesus said unto him, No man, having put his hand to the plough, and looking back, is fit for the kingdom of God."

B. Could Jesus be too harsh on these demands? He knows that:

1. if you delay your decision to follow the Lord, there will be no commitment
2. you are giving the enemy a chance to alter your situation, you will doubt, and be unsettled to serve God
3. there will be no determination to follow through and experience all that God wants you to do to transform your life (Rom. 12:2)

C. Allow God to plough and reveal his intentions as Paul personally states:

- Philippians 3:13-14, "Brethren, I count not myself to have <u>apprehended</u>: but this one thing I do, <u>forgetting those things which are behind, and reaching forth unto those things which are before, I press toward</u> the mark for the prize of the high calling of God in Christ Jesus."
Paul plans to:
1. push forward

2. plan ahead

3. let the Holy Spirit lead

D. Serving God someday is not a plan. The farmer knows without the whole field planted, there will be no harvest.

- James 2:17-19, "Even so faith, if it <u>hath not works, is dead</u>, being alone. Yea, a man may say, Thou hast faith, and I have works: shew me thy faith without thy works, and I will <u>shew thee my faith by my works</u>. Thou believest that there is one God; thou doest well: the devils also believe, and tremble."

II. Today has come.

The past is too late.

A. Time gets away from us all; before you know it, the future has become the past.
   1. you can look back on your life and experience
   2. you can regret some decisions
   3. you can't change the past, but the future is now
B. What would your life be now as a surrendered human being?

- Luke 9:23-24, "And he said to them all, If any man will come after me, <u>let him deny himself</u>, and <u>take up his cross daily, and follow me</u>. For whosoever will <u>save his life shall lose it</u>: but whosoever will <u>lose his life for my sake, the same shall save it</u>."
   1. could decisions have been made differently
   2. did God want you to step out in faith and trust him

C. The high road is less traveled because Christians tend to walk by sight and not by faith.

- II Corinthians 5:7, "For we walk by faith, not by sight."

D. Some go to church and hear the word, some go and are distracted. This appears to be a mystery why some are inspired while others are not moved by the preaching of God's word.

- Luke 8:5-8, "A sower went out to sow his seed: and as he sowed, some <u>fell by the way side</u>; and it was trodden down, and the fowls of the air devoured it. And some <u>fell upon a rock</u>; and as soon as it was sprung up, <u>it withered away</u>, because it lacked moisture. And some fell <u>among thorns</u>; and the thorns sprang up with it, and <u>choked it</u>. And other <u>fell on good ground</u>, and sprang up, and <u>bare fruit an hundredfold</u>. And when he had said these things, he cried, He that <u>hath ears to hear, let him hear</u>."

E. Some will go to church for their weekly fix and not enough inspiration to change their life.

A wise sower will choose the good ground, as Jesus explains:

- Luke 8:15, "But that on the good ground are they, which in an <u>honest and good heart</u>, having <u>heard the word, keep it, and bring forth fruit with patience</u>."
  1. listen to glean truth
  2. intend to take away knowledge
  3. let God inspire through his word

- Matthew 5:6, "Blessed are they which do <u>hunger and thirst after righteousness: for they shall be filled</u>."

III. Your new walk.
Do it on purpose.

A. True conversion will be obvious to the believer and those around.
   1. toying with the facts bring no change
   2. you don't gradually get saved
   3. born-again will be an undeniable change
   4. let your light shine

- Luke 8:16-18, "No man, when he hath lighted a candle, covereth it with a vessel, or putteth it under a bed; but <u>setteth it on a candlestick</u>, that they which enter in may see the light. For nothing is secret, that shall not be made manifest; neither any thing hid, that shall not be known and come abroad. Take heed therefore how ye hear: for whosoever hath, to him shall be given; and whosoever hath not, from him shall be taken even that which he seemeth to have."

B. A serious commitment will have to be made at some point
   1. the Holy Spirit will guide you
   2. the Holy Spirit will encourage you
   3. the Holy Spirit will strengthen you

   - Galatians 5:16-17, "This I say then, Walk in the Spirit, and ye shall not fulfill the lust of the flesh. For the flesh lusteth against the Spirit, and the Spirit against the flesh: and these are contrary the one to the other: so that ye cannot do the things that ye would."

C. You will have good intentions, but will still face a battle with your flesh.

   Your challenge:

   ➤ Walk in the Spirit – A new spiritual bond with God, a new guidance by the Holy Spirit. (Paraclete)

   ➤ Ye shall not fulfill the lust of the flesh – The unity with the Spirit needs to stay intact. (Eph.4:3) Your best is to mortify the flesh. (Rom. 6:6)

   ➤ You have walked in the flesh all your life – Now there are boundaries to think about, you will gain wisdom as you walk. (Phil. 4:8)

TEST YOUR KNOWLEDGE

SECTION IV

1. Promises are broken unintentionally all the time. True ___ False ___
2. Does God want you to act promptly on your decisions to follow him? Yes ___ No ___
3. What are some reasons you can't delay from following his leading?
    a. there will be no _____
    b. the enemy can _____ your situation with _____ and unsettle you to serve God
    c. you won't experience all that God wants you to do to _____ ___ your life
4. Complete these verses found in Philippians 3:13-14 – "Brethren, I count not myself not to have _____: but this one thing I do, _____ those which are _____, and _____ forth unto those things which are _____, I _____ toward the mark for the prize of the _____ _____ of God in Christ Jesus."
5. Serving God some days is a good plan. True ___ False ___ "Even so faith, if it hath not _____, is _____, being alone." (Jam. 2:17)
6. The high road is the less traveled because Christians walk by _____ and not by _____.
7. Distractions can be a detriment to inspiration of the hearing of God's word preached. True ___ False ___
8. In Jesus' parable of the sower of Luke chapter 8, where did the seeds fall?
    a. by the _____; trodden down and the fowls devoured
    b. upon a _____; withered away because it lacked moisture
    c. among _____; choked it out

    d. good _____; became fruitful

9. Complete this verse found in Luke 8:8c, "…He that hath _____ to hear, let him _____."

10. Once a person gets saved, Jesus likens you to a what in Luke 8:16-18? A _____

11. Walk in the Spirit and "ye shall not fulfill the _____ of the _____."

12. When a new believer commits to serving God, the Holy Spirit will:

    a. g_____ you
    b. e_____ you
    c. s_____ you

Take the High Road

Doing the Right Thing

When the Devil is Camped Outside Your Door

Section V

- ❖ The Enemy Shows Up
- ❖ The Sinful Truth
- ❖ Approach to the Battle
- ❖ The Great Lie

I. The enemy shows up.

    A. King Hezekiah had a personal walk with God and an honorable kingdom. Things seemed to be going well.

- II Chronicles 31:20-21, "And thus did Hezekiah throughout all Judah, and wrought that which was <u>good and right and</u> <u>truth before the Lord his God</u>. And in every work that he began in the service of the house of God, and in the law, and in the commandments, to seek his God, he did it with <u>all his heart, and prospered</u>."

    B. All Christians will at times be faced with insurmountable odds as Hezekiah.

- II Chronicles 32:1, "After these things, and the establishment thereof, Sennacherib king of Assyria came, and entered into Judah, and encamped against the fenced cities, and <u>thought to win them for himself.</u>" (army of 200,000)

C. Hezekiah had a plan of action to save his people.

- II Chronicles 32:3-4, "<u>He took counsel with his princes and his mighty men to stop the waters of the fountains</u> which were without the city: and they did help him. So there was gathered much people together, <u>who stopped all the fountains, and the brook that ran through the midst of the land</u>, saying, Why should the kings of Assyria come, and find much water?"

D. True wisdom is living your life under God's protection because the enemy is always lurking to find a weakness.

- I Peter 5:8-9, "<u>Be sober,</u> <u>be vigilant</u>; because your adversary the devil, as a roaring lion, walketh about, <u>seeking whom he may devour</u>: <u>Whom resist steadfast in the faith,</u> knowing that the same afflictions are accomplished in your brethren that are in the world."
  1. the devil will always be against God and test his boundaries, and if your are standing with God, you will be tested as well
  2. ignoring the enemy does not make him go away, it just leaves you defenseless

E. What happens to the person who knows his sin that so easily besets him, and chooses to not deal with it? Be wise:
  1. don't leave your life vulnerable in any area
  2. the enemy is trying to stop your spiritual growth, don't enable him

- James 4:8, "Draw nigh to God, and he will draw nigh to you. <u>Cleanse your hands, ye sinners;</u> <u>and purify your hearts, ye double minded.</u>"

II. The sinful truth.
God sees all.

A. You might realize your own sinful state, but God sees more. He has watched the generations of your family.

- Exodus 20:5-6, "...for I the Lord thy God am a jealous God, <u>visiting the iniquity of the fathers upon the children unto the third and fourth generation</u> of them that hate me; and shewing mercy unto thousands of them that love me, and keep my commandments."

B. God has the wisdom of the ages.
   1. sin had originated in the Garden of Eden with Adam and Eve
2. the sins are carried in the blood of the original sins
3. your ancestors, at some time, have partaken and entertained sin
4. relatives died unsaved, still guilty in their sins
5. you have tendencies to be vulnerable to certain temptations. Some more than others
6. a growing Christian sees these sins and weaknesses in their body and prays for forgiveness and strength

C. Mortify the flesh.

- Romans 6:6, "Knowing this, that our old man is crucified with him, that the <u>body of sin might be destroyed</u>."

D. Total abstinence of sin, God will honor.

- Psalms 1:1-3, "Blessed is the man that walketh not in the counsel of the ungodly, nor standeth in the way of sinners, nor sitteth in the seat of the scornful. But his delight is in the law of the Lord; and in his law doth he meditate day and night. And he shall be like a tree planted by the rivers of water, that bringeth forth his fruit in his season; his leaf also shall not wither; and whatsoever he doeth shall prosper."

E. The blood of Christ reconciles.

- Ephesians 2:16, "And that he might reconcile both unto God in one body by the cross, having slain the enmity thereby."

III. Approach to the battle.
Two ways of thinking.

A. Sennacherib, King of Assyria, tries to politicize the situation.

- II Chronicles 32:10-11, "Thus saith Sennacherib king of Assyria, Whereon do ye trust, that ye abide in the siege in Jerusalem? Doth not Hezekiah persuade you to give over yourselves to die by famine and by thirst, saying, The Lord our God shall deliver us out of the hand of the king of Assyria?"
1. he was trying to place doubt in their minds about God
2. he was using fear with people of faith

B. Look at the past and don't take the losing side.

- II Chronicles 32:15-16, "Now therefore let not Hezekiah deceive you, nor persuade you on this manner, neither yet believe him: for no god of any nation or kingdom

was able to <u>deliver his people out of mine hand</u>, and out of the hand of my fathers: <u>how much less shall your God deliver you out of mine hand</u>? And his servants spake yet more against the Lord God, and against his servant Hezekiah."
- 1. the enemy has the world convinced that the goal of this life depends on:
     a. finances
     b. fame
     c. power
  2. the future doesn't depend on fleshly victories of the past

C. This worldly, devil-motivated society has an end.

- I John 2:17, "And the world <u>passeth away</u>, and the <u>lust thereof</u>: but he that doeth the will of God <u>abideth for ever</u>."

D. The world's influence is difficult to resist, but the Christian is no longer of this world.

- Philippians 2:13-16, "For it is God which worketh in you both to will and to <u>do of his good pleasure</u>. <u>Do all things without murmurings and disputings</u>: that ye may be <u>blameless and harmless</u>, <u>the sons of God</u>, without rebuke, in the midst of a <u>crooked and perverse nation</u>, among whom <u>ye shine as lights in the world</u>; Holding forth the word of life; that I may rejoice in the day of Christ, that I have not run in vain, neither labored in vain."
  1. God will get the victory and last say
  2. Christians need to rely on God's hope
  3. continue to shine as lights in a dark and perverse world

E. Now Hezekiah and Isaiah prayed to God because of this blasphemous and dangerous situation.

- II Chronicles 32:21, "And the <u>Lord sent an angel, which cut off all the mighty men of valour,</u> and <u>the leaders and captains in the camp of the king of Assyria</u>. So he returned with shame of face to his own land. And when he was come into the house of his god, they that came forth of his own bowels <u>slew him there with the sword</u>."
   1. history records that 185,000 Assyrian soldiers died from the Bubonic plague carried by field mice
   2. God can use the smallest object to bring down the largest threat

F. Approach your situation by prayer and faith.

- James 4:7, "<u>Submit yourselves</u> therefore to God. <u>Resist the devil,</u> and he will <u>flee from you</u>."

IV. The great lie.
Sin in the balance.

A. The enemy wants the Christian to willfully disobey or change God's instructions, which humanizes it.

- James 4:17, "Therefore to him that <u>knoweth to do good</u>, and <u>doeth it not</u>, to him it is sin."

B. The original sin took place with Eve being confronted by the devil.

- Genesis 3:1-5, "Now the serpent was more subtil than any beast of the field which the Lord God had made. And he said unto the woman, Yea, hath God said, Ye shall not eat of every tree of the garden? And the woman said unto the serpent, We may eat of the fruit of the trees of the garden: but of the fruit of the tree which is in the <u>midst of the garden, God hath said, Ye shall not eat of it, neither shall ye touch it, lest ye die</u>. And the serpent said unto the woman, Ye shall not surely die: for God doth know that in the day ye eat thereof, <u>then your eyes shall be opened, and ye shall be as gods, knowing good and evil</u>."

    A closer look:
- ➢ The persuasion to question God – vs. 4, "Ye shall not surely die."
- ➢ The mistranslation of God's word – vs. 3, "…neither shall ye touch it." One would conclude, that if Eve hadn't misquoted God, would the serpent have seen another way to tempt Eve?
- ➢ What would the enemy present to the Christian that sounds so alluring that one would change God's instruction?

C. Is serving God and doing the right thing too difficult for today's Christian, or should we look for the easy way out?

- ▪ Hebrews 12:1-3, "Wherefore seeing <u>we also are compassed about with so great a cloud of witnesses</u>, let us <u>lay aside every weight, and the sin which doth so easily beset us</u>, and let us <u>run with patience the race that is set before us</u>, Looking unto Jesus the author and finisher of our faith; who for the joy that was set before him <u>endured the cross</u>, despising the shame, and is set down at the right hand of the throne of God. For <u>consider him that endured such contradiction of sinners against himself, lest ye be weary and faint in your minds</u>."

D. The low road leads nowhere and you will die in your Sins. The high road leads against beliefs and customs of this blind world. You might experience:
   1. as Moses – the hardness of the way, leading an unruly people
   2. as Paul – the difficulty of the task, preaching to a new world
   3. as Joseph – the prosperity of the wicked, God turned the tables in his favor
   4. as the Disciples – the delay in fulfillment of desires, the spreading of the gospel

- Philippians 3:14, "I press toward the mark for the prize of the high calling of God in Christ Jesus."

TEST YOUR KNOWLEDGE

SECTION V

1. Hezekiah was known as a man that did _____ and _____ and _____ before the Lord his God. (II Chron. 31:20)
2. Name the king and his country who decided to attack and possess Judah. _____ King of _____
3. In a strategic move from Hezekiah and his kingdom, what did they do to try to stop this unwelcomed army?
    a. they called their neighbors to help fight ____
    b. they stopped the fountains of water _____
    c. none of the above ____
4. True wisdom is living your life under God's protection.
    True ___ False ___
5. Complete this verse found in I Peter 5:8, "Be _____, be _____; because your adversary the _____, as a roaring lion, walketh about, _____ whom he may devour."
6. God has watched your family and sees the iniquity upon the _____ and _____ generations.
7. Can a growing Christian see his/her sinful tendencies in their own flesh that is considered the sin that so easily besets them? Yes ___ No ___
8. Is it possible to inherit these sinful tendencies? Yes ___ No ___
9. Complete this verse found in Romans 6:6, "Knowing this, that our _____ _____ is crucified with him, that the _____ of _____ might be destroyed."
10. Sennacherib tried to turn the people of Jerusalem away from God by using tactics of; d_____ and f_____ in their minds.
11. Hezekiah and the prophet Isaiah prayed and cried to heaven, so God did what?
_____ (II Chron. 32:21)

12. History records that 185,000 soldiers were killed by the _____ _____ carried by _____ _____.
13. The original sin took place when _____ was confronted by the devil.
14. Eve told the serpent that God said; "the fruit of the tree which is in the midst of the garden, God hath said, Ye shall not eat of it, neither shall ye touch it, lest ye die." What was the serpent's reply?
"_____ _____ _____ _____ _____." (Gen. 3:4)
15. Eve used her own wisdom in the statement; "neither shall ye touch it," Did Eve? (choose all that apply)
    a. add to God's instruction _____
    b. misquote God's instruction _____
    c. try to resist the serpent _____
16. The low road leads nowhere while the high road leads against the beliefs and customs of this world.
    match the following:

    Moses _____
    Paul _____
    Joseph _____
    Disciples _____

    a. God turned the tables in favor against the wicked
    b. spread the gospel instead of caring for personal desires
    c. preached to a new world that proved to be difficult
    d. led an unruly people in the hardness of the wilderness

Take the High Road

Doing the Right Thing

Who Shall Deliver Me?

Section VI

- ❖ To Whom are You Listening
- ❖ Grace and Mercy
- ❖ Wisdom from on High
- ❖ Testing

I. Everyone has a voice inside, to whom are you listening?

A. If you are saved, the voice of the Holy Spirit is trying to guide you into doing the right thing.

- Romans 7:15, "<u>For that which I do I allow not</u>: for what I would, that do I not; but what I hate, that do I."

B. Why do we fight ourselves?

- Romans 7:18, "For I know that in me (<u>that is, in my flesh</u>) <u>dwelleth no good thing</u>: for to will is present with me; but how to perform that which is good <u>I find not</u>."

1. you are a three part person – not two part, as it seems (trichotomy)
   a. body – flesh desiring all things to satisfy
   b. soul – the middle where the final decisions are determined
   c. spirit – the controlling factor of the results

2. before saved, you <u>acted</u> with two parts:
   a. the spirit – considered as the "spirit of man" (I Cor. 2:11)
   b. the body – if it feels good, do it (dwelleth no good thing that profits)

3. when the Holy Spirit enters at salvation:
   a. the spirit has become regenerated – the Paraclete has come to help
   b. the soul is the part of you that has always filtered good and bad (the inner man) – stagnant before; now flowing with the "mind of Christ" (I Cor. 2:16)
   c. the body will sin or not, determined by whom you have yielded to – the spirit of man or the Spirit of God (Rom. 6:16)

C. The devil didn't concern himself with an unsaved, blind, hell-bound sinner; but now he wants to keep you in the flesh (body) as much as he can.
   1. you can't glorify God in the flesh
   2. you are distracted by the struggle of flesh and spirit

- Romans 7:24, "<u>O wretched man that I am</u>! who shall deliver me from the body of this death?"

D. The victory comes when you decide to serve Christ with the mind of Christ. The soul (mind, will, and emotions) will decide this.

- Romans 7:25, "I thank God through Jesus Christ our Lord. So then <u>with the mind</u> I myself serve the <u>law of God</u>; but <u>with the flesh the law of sin</u>."

II. Grace and Mercy.
When you make the wrong decisions.

A. But I want to be spiritual, and serve God, and be victorious, but I am being defeated.

- Romans 7:22-23, "For I delight in the law of God after the inward man: But I see another law in my members, <u>warring against the law of my mind</u>, and <u>bringing me into captivity to the law of sin</u> which is in my members."

B. This struggle can become overwhelming on our own.

- Hebrews 4:16, "Let us <u>therefore come boldly</u> unto the throne of grace, that we may obtain <u>mercy</u>, and find <u>grace to help in time of need</u>."

C. Society has a dangerous saying today; "The heart wants what it wants."
   1. this is meant to be a license to sin
   2. you will find yourself in want
   3. decisions can't be directed by faith

- Jeremiah 17:9, "The heart is <u>deceitful</u> above all things, and <u>desperately wicked</u>: who can know it?"

D. The prodigal son made the decision to strike out on his own and the father divided his living unto him."

- Luke 15:13-14, "And not many days after the younger son gathered all together, and took his journey into a far country, and there <u>wasted his substance with riotous living</u>. And when he had <u>spent all</u>, there arose a mighty famine in the land; and <u>he began to be in want</u>."
    1. Who knew a famine would come?
    2. he had already wasted his substance

E. No way to recover?

- Luke 15:15-16, "And he went and joined himself to a citizen of that country; and he sent him into his fields to feed swine. <u>And he would fain have filled his belly</u> with the husks that the swine did eat: <u>and no man gave unto him</u>."
    1. joined himself to a strange citizen in a strange land
    2. he got a job that paid what
    3. a Jewish boy feeding swine
    4. the low road became the bottom

F. There is pleasure in sin for a season. (Heb. 11:25)

Sin will take you farther than you want to go, keep you longer than you want to stay, and cost you more than you want to pay.

G. The decision of repentance.

- Luke 15:18-19, "I will <u>arise and go to my father</u>, and will say unto him, <u>Father, I have sinned against heaven</u>, and <u>before thee</u>, And am no more worthy to be called thy son: make me as one of thy hired servants."

H. Desperation is not planned; it will bring us to our knees before the almighty to cry for help and mercy.

- Psalms 139:1-4, "<u>O Lord, thou hast searched me, and known me</u>. Thou knowest my downsitting and mine uprising, thou understandest my thought afar off. Thou compassest my path and my lying down, and art acquainted with all my ways. For there is not a word in my tongue, but, lo, O Lord, thou knowest it altogether."

I. A person can be their own worst enemy. Peter had good intentions, but Jesus saw something else.

- Luke 22:34, "And he said, I tell thee, Peter, the cock shall not crow this day, before that thou shalt thrice deny <u>that thou knowest me</u>."
  1. we all have times of weakness
  2. only the grace and mercy of God sets us right again

III. Wisdom from on high.
God knows our inward man.

A. The world offers false security as the rulers plan their wisdom.

- Psalms 2:4, "He that sitteth in the heavens shall laugh: the Lord shall have them in derision."
  1. the kings and rulers rely on their wisdom
  2. they shall stammer

B. The Christian has a tendency to be independent in thinking also and not considering the Lord. Jesus said;

- Luke 11:23, "He that is <u>not with me</u> <u>is against me</u>: and he that <u>gathereth not</u> with me <u>scattereth</u>."
  1. If you are not sold out for the Lord

      2. if you are going against the Lord's intentions
      3. this leaves no middle ground – high or low

C. What are my weaknesses and how could God use a person like me?

- Psalms 139:16, "Thine eyes did see my substance, yet <u>being unperfect</u>; and <u>in thy book</u> all my members were <u>written</u>, which in continuance were <u>fashioned</u>, when as yet there was none of them."
  1. he saw me before I was created
  2. he fashioned me and I am imperfect

D. Your body does what your mind tells it to. How much does the law of God mean to you?

- Romans 7:22, "For I <u>delight</u> in the law of God after the inward man."

E. You could be misdirected as Saul of Tarsus thought by his inward man to wipe out the early church.

- Acts 8:3-4, "As for Saul, he <u>made havock of the church</u>, entering into every house, and <u>haling men and women committed them to prison</u>. Therefore they that were scattered abroad went <u>every where preaching the word</u>."
  1. this rabbi knew he was serving God
  2. he had a great zeal for his mission (sold out)
  3. the Christians that were scattered were the <u>real servants of God</u>

- Proverbs 23:7, "For as he thinketh in his heart, so is he…"

F. Saul seemed unstoppable by his inward drive.

- Acts 9:1-2; "And Saul, yet <u>breathing out threatenings and slaughter against the disciples of the Lord,</u> went unto the high priest, And desired of him letters to Damascus to the synagogues, that if he found <u>any of this way</u>, whether they were men or women, he might bring them <u>bound</u> unto Jerusalem."

G. Enough is enough, the road ends here.

- Acts 9:3-6, "And as he journeyed, he came near Damascus: and suddenly there shined round about him a <u>light from heaven</u>: And he fell to the earth, and heard a voice saying unto him, <u>Saul, Saul, why persecutest thou me</u>? And he said, Who art thou, Lord? And the Lord said, <u>I am Jesus whom thou persecutest</u>: it is hard for thee to <u>kick against the pricks</u>. And he trembling and astonished said, Lord, <u>what wilt thou have me to do</u>? And the Lord said unto him, Arise, and go into the city, and it shall be told thee <u>what thou must do</u>."

    1. his misdirection comes to an abrupt stop
    2. Saul was wrong all the time, but committed
    3. a person still can be used of God

IV. Testing.
The teacher is on your side.

A. Nobody likes a test, especially from the Lord.

- Hebrews 12:6, "For whom the Lord <u>loveth</u> he <u>chasteneth</u>, and <u>scourgeth</u> every son whom he <u>receiveth</u>."

B. Somewhere in your inward man you know you need to be set straight, to start on the best path.

- Hebrews 12:11-14; "Now no chastening for the present seemeth to be joyous, but <u>grievous</u>: nevertheless afterward it yiedeth the peaceable fruit of <u>righteousness</u> unto them which are exercised thereby. Wherefore lift up the hands which hang down, and the feeble knees; And <u>make straight paths for your feet</u>, lest that which is lame be turned out of the way; but let it rather <u>be healed</u>. <u>Follow peace with all men, and holiness, without which no man shall see the Lord</u>."
  1. spiritual boot camp is not fun, but necessary
  2. the prize is yielding righteousness
  3. the path will show you the Lord working in you

C. There is great value in the Lord's correction.

- Hebrews 12:9, "Furthermore we have had fathers of our flesh which corrected us, and we gave them <u>reverence</u>: shall we not much rather be in <u>subjection unto the Father of spirits, and live</u>?"

D. Would a person neglect God's teachings and act in the flesh as Esau did?

- Hebrews 12:15-16, "Looking diligently lest any man <u>fail of the grace of God</u>; lest any <u>root of bitterness springing up trouble you</u>, and thereby many be defiled; Lest there be any fornicator, or profane person, as Esau, who for one morsel of meat <u>sold his birthright</u>."

E. The fact that Jesus died for your sins to give you a new life needs to stay in your thinking and gratefulness.

- II Corinthians 10:5, "<u>Casting down imaginations</u>, and <u>every high thing</u> that exalteth itself <u>against the</u>

knowledge of God, and bringing into captivity every thought to the obedience of Christ."
1. don't treat God's grace with disrespect
2. don't let your flesh challenge the Holy Spirit
3. keep all thoughts in obedience

F. What you will it to be, it will be. Freedom is yours.

- Romans 8:2, "For the law of the Spirit of life in Christ Jesus hath made me free from the law of sin and death."

TEST YOUR KNOWLEDGE

SECTION VI

1. You are a three part person, a trichotomy, consisting of:
    a. _____ - the flesh desiring all things to satisfy
    b. _____ - the middle where the final decisions are determined
    c. _____ - the controlling factor of the result
2. The soul has always chosen the right thing. True ___ False ___
3. The body will sin or not determined by your listening to the _____ of man or the _____ of God.
4. Complete this verse found in Romans 7:24, _ "O _____ man that I am! who shall _____ me from the _____ of this _____?"
5. With the mind I serve the law of God and with the mind I serve the law of sin. True ___ False ___
6. Complete this verse found in Jeremiah 17:9, "The heart is _____ above all things, and _____ _____: who can know it?"
7. Luke chapter fifteen tells of a young man who decided to take his inheritance and leave the country.
List his events in order. (a, b, c, d, e)
    ___ famine arose in the land
    ___ he wasted his substance on riotous living
    ___ he returned home to his father
    ___ he fed the pigs
    ___ he joined himself with a stranger
8. Sin will t____ you f____ than you w____ to go, m____ you s____ l____ than you want to s____, and c____ you m____ than you want to p____.
9. God knows that I am not perfect, so he can't work with me. True ___ False ___

10. Who was the individual threatening the early Church in Acts 8? _____ of _____

11. When the Church scattered, these Christians went everywhere; (check one)
    a. to find a place to hide _____
    b. start a new religion _____
    c. preaching the word _____

12. Who got the misdirected servant's attention on the road to Damascus? _____

13. Complete this verse found in Hebrews 12:6 – "For whom the Lord _____ he _____, and _____ every son whom he _____."

14. Who neglected God and gave up his birthright for one morsel of meat, according to Hebrews 12:16? _____

15. All Christians should stay in the thinking of gratefulness. True _____ False _____

16. Complete this verse found in II Corinthians 10:5 – "Casting down _____, and every _____ _____ that _____ itself _____ the _____ of God, and bringing into _____ every _____ to the _____ of Christ."

Take the High Road

Doing the Right Thing

Do Not Lust

Section VII

- ❖ Conquering Lust
- ❖ A Spiritual Compromise
- ❖ Lust Lingers
- ❖ Satisfaction of the Soul

I. Conquering the lust.

A. How does God see the severity of lust in a Christian's life?

- Matthew 5:28, "But I say unto you, that whosoever <u>looketh on a woman to lust after her</u> hath committed <u>adultery</u> with her already in his heart."
  1. the act of adultery doesn't need to be performed by the body
  2. the flesh is still at fault

- Matthew 5:29-30, "And if thy right eye offend thee, <u>pluck it out</u>, and cast it from thee: for it is <u>profitable for thee</u> that one of thy members should <u>perish</u>, and not that thy <u>whole body</u> should be <u>cast into hell</u>. And if thy right hand offend thee, <u>cut it off</u>, and cast it from thee: for it is profitable for thee that one of thy members

should perish, and not that thy whole body should be <u>cast into hell</u>."
1. Should a person go through life with body parts missing?
2. the law requires severe consequences for sin
3. the salvation of Christ saves you from eternity in hell

B. The eye is figurative of spiritual light and darkness.

- Matthew 6:22-23, "<u>The light of the body is the eye</u>: if therefore thine <u>eye be single</u>, thy whole body shall be <u>full of light</u>. But if thine eye be <u>evil</u>, thy whole body shall be full of <u>darkness</u>. If therefore the light that is in thee be darkness, <u>how great is that darkness</u>!"

C. The lusting of the eyes is the greatest delusion because of:
1. spiritual immorality – James 1:14, tempted by lust
2. blindness to reality – Romans 14:7-8, can't live to yourself
3. constant self offense – Matthew 5:29, try to train your focus

   Closer look:
   ➢ If thy right eye "offend" thee, pluck it out. The word for offend in the Greek is, "skandalizo;" to entrap; where we get the English word "scandal."

D. Jesus' choice of words referring to the "right hand" and the "right eye," significantly means:
1. what the right eye desires, the right hand will act it out
2. what we look for, we see, and this will affect the heart
3. when the heart is affected, the flesh will act out
   a. the Spirit – pneuma – influenced by God or Satan (who you listen to)

      b. the soul – psuche – influenced by the Spirit (mind, will, and emotions)
      c. the body – soma- influenced by the soul (the body will sin)

E. Lust is a willful violation originated by Satan; focus on God.

- Proverbs 4:23-27, "<u>Keep thy heart with all diligence</u>; for out of it are the <u>issues of life</u>. Put away from thee a <u>froward mouth</u>, and <u>perverse lips</u> put far from thee. Let thine <u>eyes look right on</u>, and let <u>thine eyelids look straight</u> before thee. <u>Ponder the path of thy feet</u>, and let all thy ways be <u>established</u>. Turn no to the right hand nor to the left: remove thy foot from <u>evil</u>."

II. A Spiritual compromise.
Old self with new self.

A. When one compares the life of Samson and Daniel, you can see quite a difference between these two God-chosen men.

- Samson – rejected God's Law on marriage and ended up losing his supernatural strength because of a heathen woman.
- Daniel – decided to follow the Law of God, even though it may have cost his life, refusing authority and publicly praying three times daily.
- Samson – had his eyes and mind on the ladies and demanded his parents to help him fulfill his lust.
- Daniel – had his eyes and mind on the Lord on spiritual matters and spiritual visions.
- Samson – Samson – refused to follow his childhood training, he was rebellious.

- Daniel – followed his childhood training and brought glory to God and his people.
- Samson – his physical lust and appetite resulted in being blinded, enslaved, and death.
- Daniel – had self-control over physical appetites and God honored him at the lions' den, and by the kingdom.

B. Look at your old self and compare with your new self and what you see God is doing to change you as you yield to him.

- Romans 12:1, "I beseech you therefore, brethren, by the mercies of God, that ye <u>present your bodies a living sacrifice,</u> <u>holy, acceptable unto God</u>, which is your <u>reasonable service.</u>"

C. Following the instruction of this renewal requires transformation.

- Romans 12:2, "And be not <u>conformed</u> to this world: but be ye <u>transformed by the renewing of your mind</u>, that ye may prove what is that good, and <u>acceptable</u>, and <u>perfect</u>, will of God."

Closer look:
> to "renew" your mind is the Greek word, "anakainosis," which means to renovate; this has to take place to "prove" what is acceptable unto God, is the Greek word, "dakimazo," which means to examine, discern, try; God can see your falsehoods, you can too

D. Plan your work, then work your plan; like a remodel.

1. carefully write down everything that needs work

    2. start one by one to conquer these areas with the least temptations
    3. realize that when you are faced with the sin that "so easily besets you," the enemy will fight you
    4. present yourself humbly before God, and let the Holy Spirit guide you to stand against the wiles of the devil (Armor of God, Eph. 6)
    5. constant renewing on a daily basis by prayer and the washing of God's word; pray, read, memorize the Bible
    6. take an assessment of what your new Renovation looks like now, and thank God for the victories
    7. determine to serve the Lord in this new spiritual strength and wisdom

- Philippians 3:7-8, "But what things were gain to me, those I counted <u>loss for Christ</u>. Yea doubtless, and I count all things but loss for the <u>excellency of the knowledge of Christ Jesus my Lord</u>: for whom I have <u>suffered the loss</u> of all things, and do count them but dung, that <u>I may win Christ</u>."

III. Lust lingers.
Temptations are still present.

A. Can you fall prey to lust unintentionally?

- Proverbs 6:27-28, "Can a man take fire in his bosom, and his clothes <u>not be burned</u>? Can one go upon hot coals, and his feet <u>not be burned</u>?"
  1. the mind can play tricks on your temptations
  2. the senses can replay the pleasures of taste, smell, and sounds that take you back to the past

B. Temptations can have a diverse effect on the unprepared Christian.

- I Peter 5:8-10, "Be sober, be vigilant; because your adversary the devil, as a roaring lion, walketh about, seeking whom he may devour: whom resist steadfast in the faith, knowing that the same afflictions are accomplished in your brethren that are in the world. But the God of all grace, who hath called us unto his eternal glory by Christ Jesus, after that ye have suffered a while, make you perfect, stablish, strengthen, settle you."

C. Friends can lead you in the wrong direction.
   1. friends can go along with anything worldly
   2. friends can be saved, but are "carnal Christians"
   3. the separation of the unsaved friends should be seriously considered when you witnessed to them with no response

   - I Corinthians 15:33-34, "Be not deceived: evil communications corrupt good manners. Awake to righteousness, and sin not; for some have not the knowledge of God: I speak this to your shame."

IV. Satisfaction of the soul.
Restrain the flesh.

A. The flesh has an insatiable drive that controls a person even if he has wisdom to resist.
   1. Esau sold his birthright for a bowl of stew (Gen. 25:30)
   2. the woman at the well had multiple husbands (John 4:18)
      a. Jesus promised her water that is everlasting
      b. never thirst again

B. The unsaved have no restraint, whereas the believer has the Holy Spirit's strength.

- Isaiah 58:11, "And the Lord <u>shall guide thee continually</u>, and satisfy thy soul in drought, and make fat thy bones: and thou shalt be like a watered garden, and like a spring of water, whose <u>waters fail not</u>."

C. When we are tried of God, his presence is undeniable as Job found out.

- Job 42:2-3, "I know that thou <u>canst do every thing</u>, and that <u>no thought can be withholden from thee</u>. Who is he that hideth counsel without knowledge? therefore have I uttered that <u>I understood not</u>; things too wonderful for me, which I knew not."

D. How can I know peace? When sin is present there is guilt and unrest, no inner peace.

- I John 1:9, "If we <u>confess our sins</u>, he is faithful and just to forgive us our sins, and to <u>cleanse us from all unrighteousness</u>."
    1. God will forgive and bring us back to fellowship with him
    2. this roller coaster is not a true walk with God
    3. there is never a lasting peace with this arrangement

E. The spirit is ever present to bring you wisdom in times of lust and weakness.

- Proverbs 2:10-11, "<u>When wisdom entereth into thine heart</u>, and <u>knowledge is pleasant unto thy soul</u>; <u>Discretion shall preserve thee</u>, <u>understanding shall keep thee</u>."

F. It is difficult to turn from your lust and weaknesses, but turn your focus on bringing fruit from your spiritual life.

- Galatians 5:22-25, "But the fruit of the Spirit is love, joy, peace, longsuffering, gentleness, goodness, faith, meekness, temperance: against such there is no law. And they that are Christ's have <u>crucified the flesh</u> with the <u>affections and lusts</u>. If <u>we live in the Spirit</u>, let us also <u>walk in the Spirit</u>."

TEST YOUR KNOWLEDGE

SECTION VII

1. Does God see lust as the act of sin according to Matthew 5:28? Yes ___ No ___
2. Can the flesh be at fault even though the body has not performed the act, such as adultery? Yes ___ No ___
3. Complete these verses found in Matthew 6:22-23 – "The _____ of the body is the _____: if therefore thine _____ be single, thy whole body shall be _____ of _____. But if thine _____ be evil, thy whole body shall be full of _____. If therefore the light that is in thee be _____, how _____ is that _____!"
4. The lusting of the eyes is the greatest delusion because of:
    a. spiritual immorality ____
    b. blindness to reality ____
    c. constant self-offense ____
    d. all of the above ____
5. When the body is influenced by the soul, the body will sin or not sin. True ___ False ___
6. Lust is a willful _____ originated by Satan.
7. Complete this verse found in Proverbs 4:23 – "Keep thy _____ with all _____; for out of it are the _____ of life."
8. Daniel and Samson were both considered men chosen by God to fulfill his purpose. When confronted with lust, one man <u>gave in to self</u> and the other <u>gave in to God</u>.
    Choose which:
    Samson _____
    Daniel _____
9. Romans 12:2 tells us to be not c_____ to this world but be t_____ by the renewing of the mind.
10. Plan your work then _____ _____ _____.

11. Complete these verses found in Proverbs 6:27-28 – "Can a man take _____ in his bosom, and his clothes not be _____?" "Can one go upon hot coals, and his feet not be _____?"

12. True or false; the senses can bring back temptations from the past by smell, taste, and sound. True ____ False ____

13. Friends can have a great impact on your life. If your friend is not saved and doesn't want to hear you, will this hurt your walk with God? Yes ___ No ___

14. Complete this verse found in I Corinthians 15:33 – "Be not deceived: evil _____ corrupt _____ _____."

15. List the nine fruits of the Spirit found in Galatians 5:22-23 –
   ➤ _____   _____   _____
   ➤ _____   _____   _____
   ➤ _____   _____   _____

   "...against such there is no law."

Take the High Road

Doing the Right Thing

Our Rock of Offence

Section VIII

- ❖ A Rock of Offence
- ❖ God Can Shape You
- ❖ Jesus is Our Rock

I. A Rock of offence.

A. The new Pharaoh did not know Joseph and couldn't accept God's hand on this Hebrew people.

- Exodus 1:8-10, "Now there arose up a new king over Egypt, which <u>knew not Joseph</u>. And he said unto his people, Behold, the people of the children of Israel are <u>more and mightier than we</u>: Come on, let us <u>deal wisely with them</u>; lest they multiply, and it come to pass, that, when there falleth out any war, they join also unto our enemies, and <u>fight against us</u>, and so get them up out of the land."
    1. should you make this people an ally
    2. should you overtake with authority

B. Egypt's action plan backfires.

- Exodus 1:11-12, "Therefore they did set over them <u>taskmasters to afflict them</u> with their burdens. And they built for Pharaoh treasure cities, Pithom and Raamses. But the more they <u>afflicted them</u>, the more they <u>multiplied</u> <u>and grew</u>. And they were grieved because of the children of Israel."
  1. society's plan today is to limit and oppress Christians
  2. history proves that God's people multiply under oppression
  3. these people have become a stumbling block to Egypt
  4. Pharaoh has adopted an attitude of destructive behavior
  5. his sin of aggression toward God and Israel could mean annihilation

C. A rock of offence that the world does not know how to handle whose name is Jesus Christ.

- I Peter 2:8, "And a <u>stone of stumbling</u>, and <u>a rock of offence</u>, even to them which <u>stumble at the word</u>, being disobedient: whereunto they also were appointed."

D. God has a plan for the world whether people believe or not. Jesus is the plan for mankind, not the agenda of the world.

- Psalms 53:1, "<u>The fool</u> hath said in <u>his heart</u>, <u>There is no God</u>. Corrupt are they, and have done <u>abominable iniquity</u>: there is <u>none</u> that doeth good."
- I Peter 2:7, "Unto you therefore which <u>believe</u> he is <u>precious</u>: but unto them which be disobedient, the stone which the <u>builders disallowed</u>, the same is made the <u>head of the corner</u>."

E. The rock has been smitten for the people.

- Exodus 17:4-6, "And Moses cried unto the Lord, saying, What shall I do unto this people? they be almost ready to stone me. And the Lord said unto Moses, Go on before the people, and take with thee of the elders of Israel; and thy rod, wherewith thou smotest the river, take in thine hand, and go. Behold, I will stand before thee there upon the rock in Horeb; and thou shalt smite the rock, and there shalt come water out of it, that the people may drink. And Moses did so in the sight of the elders of Israel."
  1. people do need water to survive
  2. even hostile people are offered the water
  3. Jesus is our rock to sustain life
  4. he was smitten when crucified for our sins

F. When the walk with God gets challenging, should the believers allow themselves to be angry and hostile?

- Exodus 17:7, "And he called the name of that place Massah, and Meribah, because of the chiding of the children of Israel, and because they tempted the Lord, saying, Is the Lord among us, or not?"

II. God can shape you.
Yield to the challenge.

A. The norm today is to leave a church if conviction or challenges are present to change your life. The children of Israel were filled with hope in the beginning; the road became hard but God never failed to provide.
  1. supply was abundant – over 2 million people drank from the rock
  2. supply was lasting – they drank of the stream until they reached the promise land

3. in the presence of the Elders – these men stayed skeptical of God, and later their descendants would pay Judas to betray Jesus
4. Jesus gives the water of life freely – hanging on the cross, he was pierced in the side and water and blood came gushing out to cleanse and satisfy the thirsty soul

- Psalms 62:1-3, "Truly my soul <u>waiteth upon God</u>: from him cometh <u>my salvation</u>. <u>He only is my rock and my salvation</u>; he is my defence; I shall not be <u>greatly moved</u>. How long will ye imagine mischief against a man? ye shall be slain all of you: as a <u>bowing wall shall ye be</u>, and as a <u>tottering fence</u>."

B. The apostle Paul would reach a new outlook with his walk with God through the challenges. The ultimate gain is heaven.

- Philippians 1:21-23, "For me to <u>live is Christ</u>, and <u>to die is gain</u>. But if I live in the flesh, this is the <u>fruit of my labour</u>: yet what I shall choose I wot not. For I am in a <u>strait betwixt two</u>, having a desire to depart, and <u>to be with Christ</u>; which is <u>far better</u>."

C. When the world is closing in-- finances, health, marriage, the enemy-- hold on to the rock.

- II Timothy 2:19, "Nevertheless the <u>foundation of God standeth sure</u>, having this <u>seal</u>, The Lord <u>knoweth them</u> that are his. And, Let every one that nameth the <u>name of Christ depart from iniquity</u>."

III. Jesus is our rock.
Choose to believe.

A. Jesus has become an unmovable reality that can't be overpowered. So accept him or believe him not as the Jews did.

- John 1:11, "He came unto his own, and his own received him not."

B. Jesus admittedly came as a sword to divide people with truth.

- Matthew 10:34-39, "Think not that I am come to send peace on earth: I came not to send peace, but a sword. For I am come to set a man at variance against his father, and the daughter against her mother, and the daughter in law against her mother in law. And a man's foes shall be they of his own household. He that loveth father or mother more than me is not worthy of me: and he that loveth son or daughter more than me is not worthy of me. And he that taketh not his cross, and followeth after me, is not worthy of me. He that findeth his life shall lose it: and he that loseth his life for my sake shall find it."
    1. Christianity cannot be a spectator event to add to your life, it must replace the old one
    2. if Jesus is not all to you, he is nothing to you

TEST YOUR KNOWLEDGE

SECTION VIII

1. The new Pharaoh knew Joseph and honored God.
   True ___ False ___
2. The more the children of Israel were afflicted, the more they multiplied and grew. True ___ False ___
3. What was the main fear that Egypt had about these people?
   a. they would grow rich and overtake Egypt ___
   b. they would raise up a ruler to replace the Pharaoh ___
   c. they would side with Egypt's enemies and fight against them ___
4. Israel had become a rock of offence to Egypt.
   True ___ False ___
5. Would you say that God was a rock of offence to Egypt?
   Yes ___ No ___
6. Complete this verse found in Psalms 53:1 – "The _____ hath said in his _____, There is no _____. Corrupt are they, and have done _____ _____: there is _____ that doeth good."
7. What did Moses strike by God's command, and water came out?
   a. a golden calf ___
   b. a rock ___
   c. a water well ___
8. How many people drank from the bountiful water supply?
   a. 10,000 ___
   b. 100,000 ___
   c. 2,000,000 ___
9. In Exodus 17:7, the people said, while tempting the Lord; "Is the _____ among us, or _____?"
10. If you are not choosing to follow the Lord, you will become like a b_____ w____ or a t_____ f_____ according to Psalms 62:3.

11. The believers in Jesus Christ have become a rock of offence to the world because he is this rock. True ___ False ___

12. Complete this verse found in II Timothy 2:19 – "Nevertheless the _____ of _____ standeth _____, having this seal, The Lord knoweth them that are _____. And, Let every one that _____ the _____ of Christ depart from iniquity."

13. Where is this verse found? "He came unto his own, and his own received him not." _____

14. Jesus came not to send peace on the earth, but he came to bring a _____, according to Matthew 10:34.

15. You can add Jesus to your present life and go about your own business. True ___ False ___

"He that _____ his life shall _____ it: and he that _____ his _____ for my sake shall _____ it." (Mat. 10:39)

Take the High Road

Doing the Right Thing

How is Your Speech?

Section IX

- ❖ **Wisdom of Words**
- ❖ **Power in the Tongue**
- ❖ **Silence is Golden**

I. Wisdom of words.

A. Who is wise with their speech? What makes a person wise with their words?

- James 3:13, "Who is a wise man and endued with knowledge among you? let him shew out of a good conversation his works with meekness of wisdom."
    1. Jesus went as a sheep to the slaughter and opened not his mouth
    2. Daniel did not curse and yell as they threw him in the lions' den
    3. Job didn't curse God and die as his wife suggested
    4. Abraham never questioned God's wisdom when he was asked to offer up his own son

B. When you have chosen to take the high road with God, you will yield to the Holy Spirit even in the most challenging situation. Notice Jesus' and Stephen's last words:

- Luke 23:34, "Father, forgive them; for they know not what they do."
- Acts 7:60, "Lord, lay not this sin to their charge."

C. Why is the tongue so difficult to tame?

- James 3:8-9, "But the tongue can <u>no man tame</u>; it is an <u>unruly evil</u>, full of <u>deadly poison</u>. Therewith bless we God, even the Father; and therewith curse we men, which are made after the similitude of God."

D. Your true character will come to the surface when you speak.

- James 3:11, "Doth a fountain send forth at the same place <u>sweet water and bitter</u>?"
  1. your heart is revealed
  2. your restraint is revealed

E. What have you gave up in repentance and asked for wisdom and understanding? Lay it under the blood.

- James 3:16, "For where envying and strife is, there is <u>confusion and every evil work</u>."
  1. you have inner struggle on sin
  2. you have no peace with God on matters
  3. there could be past issues unresolved

F. What you carry inside will eat at your soul as a canker. Your heart is in the balance.

- James 3;17, "But the wisdom that is from above is first <u>pure</u>, then <u>peaceable</u>, <u>gentle</u>, and <u>easy to be intreated</u>, full of <u>mercy and good fruits</u>, without <u>partiality</u>, and without <u>hypocrisy</u>."

- Proverbs 4:23-24, "Keep thy <u>heart</u> with <u>all diligence</u>; for out of it are the <u>issues of life</u>. Put away from thee a froward mouth, and <u>perverse lips</u> put far from thee."

G. Things that are in need of attention, once you are saved, to keep your heart right:
   1. Bitterness – Hebrews 12:15, "…lest any root of bitterness springing up trouble you, and thereby many be defiled."
   2. Pride – Proverbs 13:10, "Only by pride cometh contention."
   3. Hatred – Proverbs 10:12, "Hatred stirreth up strifes: but love covereth all sins."
   4. Anger – Proverbs 14:17, "He that is soon angry dealeth foolishly…"
   5. Covetousness – Hebrews 13:5, "Let your conversation be without covetousness; and be content with such things as ye have…"
   6. Criticality – James 2:4, "Are ye not then partial in yourselves, and are become judges of evil thoughts?"

II. Power in the tongue. Blessing or cursing?

A. What good can come from the tongue? What pleases God?
   1. prayer – Paul writes to pray without ceasing. (I Thess. 5:17)
   2. witness – we share the gospel message
   3. encourage – lift up others

B. The tongue has the power to do good or bad.

- James 3:5, "Even so the tongue is a <u>little member</u>, and <u>boasteth great things</u>. Behold, how <u>great a matter</u> a little fire kindleth!"

C. Jesus knows our hearts can be defiled by our words and expose our spiritual condition when we speak.

- Matthew 12:33-37, "Either make the <u>tree good</u>, and his <u>fruit good</u>; or else make the <u>tree corrupt</u>, and his <u>fruit corrupt</u>: for the tree is known by his fruit. O generation of vipers, how can ye, being evil, speak good things? <u>for out of the</u> <u>abundance of the heart the mouth speaketh</u>. A good man out of the good treasure of the heart bringeth forth good things: and an evil man out of the evil treasure bringeth forth evil things. But I say unto you, That every idle word that men shall speak, they shall <u>give account</u> thereof in the day of judgment. For by thy words thou shalt be <u>justified</u>, and by thy words thou shalt be <u>condemned</u>."

D. Saul of Tarsus breathed out threatening and slaughter against the disciples of the Lord, but we see Paul as a different man. What changed?

- I Corinthians 9:27, "But I keep under my body, and bring it into subjection: lest that by any means, when I have preached to others, I myself should be a castaway."
  1. he accepted Christ and his heart changed
  2. he cared about people's salvation
  3. he respected the authority of the word of God
  4. he knew the power of the misspoken word; the enemy twists things
  5. the mission had to be fulfilled with a clear conscience

III. Silence is golden.
Control the tongue.

A. When there is nothing to say, say nothing. Jesus went as a lamb to the slaughter.

- Isaiah 53:7, "He was oppressed, and he was afflicted, yet he opened not his mouth: he is brought as a lamb to the slaughter…"
  1. what could he have said
     a. he came for the mission of sacrifice
     b. he overcame the emotion of setting the persecutors straight
  2. his responsibility took precedence over self

B. You can choose to say nothing rather than to argue and become bitter. No apologies necessary if you are responsible.

- James 3:14, "But if ye have bitter envying and strife in your hearts, glory not, and lie not against the truth."

C. To control the tongue, you first have to control your heart.
  1. is what you are saying glorifying God – encouragement, edifying
  2. mean what you say, and say what you mean

- Colossians 3:23, "And whatsoever ye do, do it heartily, as to the Lord, and not unto men."

- James 5:12, "But above all things, my brethren, swear not, neither by heaven, neither by the earth, neither by any other oath: but let your yea be yea; and your nay, nay; lest ye fall into condemnation."

D. The challenge of discernment and taking the high road with God, otherwise, the devil keeps you in confusing territory.

- James 3:15-17, "This wisdom descendeth not from above, but is earthly, sensual, devilish. For where envying and strife is, there is confusion and every evil work. But the wisdom that is from above is first pure, then peaceable, gentle, and easy to be intreated, full of mercy and good fruits, without partiality, and without hypocrisy."

TEST YOUR KNOWLEDGE

SECTION IX

1. Who said this very unselfish quote while dying? "Lord, lay not this sin to their charge." _____
2. James speaks of a member of the body that "no man can tame." What is this?
    a. the heart ____
    b. the tongue ____
    c. the eyes ____
3. Complete this verse found in James 3:11 – "Doth a _____ send forth at the same place _____ water and _____?"
4. Complete this verse found in Proverbs 4:23 – "Keep thy _____ with all _____; for out of it are the _____ of life."
5. There are six things that need attention to keep your heart right:
    a. b_____ (Heb. 12:15)
    b. p_____ Prov. 13:10)
    c. h_____ (Prov. 10:12)
    d. a_____ (Prov. 14:17)
    e. c_____ (Heb. 13:5)
    f. c_____ (James 2:4)
6. The tongue has the power to do good or bad. True ____ False ____
7. "For out of the abundance of the heart the mouth speaketh." Where is this verse found and who is speaking? _____, _____
8. This man breathed out threatening and slaughter against the disciples of the Lord, but changed after true salvation. What was him name when saved? _____ of _____
9. To control your tongue, you first must control your _____.
10. It is wiser to say nothing than to argue and become bitter, so controlling your tongue is a choice. True ____ False ____

Take the High Road

Doing the Right Thing

The Sin of Unbelief.

Section X

- ❖ Question of Our Belief
- ❖ The battle of Unbelief
- ❖ Love is the Proof

I. Question of our belief.

A. The children of Israel wandered in the desert for forty years because of unbelief.

- Hebrews 4:1, "Let us therefore fear, lest, a promise being left us of entering into <u>his rest</u>, any of you should seem to come short of it."

    Closer look:
    - ➤ "rest," in the Greek, "katapausis," meaning "abode"
    - ➤ some can go through the motions and seem to be saved

B. Some can hear the gospel message in the same church at the same time as someone else and not be affected.

- Hebrews 4:2-3, "For unto us was the <u>gospel preached</u>, as <u>well as unto them</u>: but the word preached did not <u>profit</u> them, not being <u>mixed with faith</u> in them that heard it. For we which have believed <u>do enter into rest</u>, as he said, As I have <u>sworn in my wrath</u>, if they shall enter into my <u>rest</u>: although the works were finished from the foundation of the world."

C. God has made a spiritual blueprint, predetermined, to carry through this present world to eternity.

- Hebrews 4:4-6, "For he spake in a certain place of the <u>seventh day</u> on this wise, And <u>God did rest the</u> <u>seventh day</u> <u>from all his works</u>. And in this place again, <u>If they shall</u> <u>enter into my rest</u>. Seeing therefore it remaineth that <u>some must enter therein,</u> and they to whom it was <u>first preached</u> <u>enter not in because of unbelief</u>."
    1. unbelief caused them to not enter into his rest
    2. God sent forth the plan, we make the choice

D. Jesus is our rest today to accept.
   1. we can enter by him
   2. we can find permanent rest

- Hebrews 4:8-9, "For if <u>Jesus had given them rest</u>, then would he not afterward have spoken of <u>another day</u>. There <u>remaineth therefore a rest</u> to the people of God."

E. We live in a world of second chances because of Jesus' finished work on the cross.

- Hebrews 4:16, "Let us therefore come <u>boldly unto the</u> <u>throne of grace</u>, that we may obtain <u>mercy</u>, and find <u>grace</u> to help in <u>time of need</u>."

II. The battle of unbelief.

A spiritual struggle.

A. We can still battle unbelief after salvation, but it leads to:

  1. <u>wasted time</u> – "Redeeming the time, because the days are evil." (Eph. 5:16)
     a. forty year march in the desert
     b. people not heeding Noah's preaching
     c. Jesus' command to follow him; "Follow me; and let the dead bury their dead." (Matt. 8:22)
  2. <u>wasted efforts</u> – "…the care of this world, and the deceitfulness of riches, choke the word, and he becometh unfruitful."(Mat. 13:22)
  "<u>No servant can serve two masters</u>: for either he will hate the one, and love the other; or else he will hold to the one, and despise the other. Ye cannot serve God and mammon." (Luke 16:13)
  3. <u>a spiritual stalemate</u> – we can't be on strike when we are so blessed; "And Elijah came unto all the people, and said, How long halt ye between two opinions? if the Lord be God, follow him: but if Baal, then follow him. And the people answered him not a word." (I Kings 18:21)

B. God has made us free in Christ Jesus.
  1. how easy it is to walk after the flesh and lose that freedom by choice
  2. we are not condemned because we are still in Christ

  - Romans 8:1, "There is therefore now <u>no condemnation</u> to them which are in Christ Jesus, <u>who walk not after the flesh, but after the Spirit</u>."

C. We choose a carnal path that the unsaved walk in. That is not of God. The Christian has been called to a higher road, a plane of victory!

- Romans 8:6-8, "<u>For to be carnally minded is death</u>: but to be <u>spiritually minded is life and peace</u>. Because the <u>carnal mind</u> is <u>enmity against God</u>: for it is not subject to the law of God, neither indeed can be. So then they that are <u>in the flesh cannot please God</u>."
  Closer look:
    - ➢ the "flesh," and "carnal," are the same Greek word "sarx"
    - ➢ the meaning is the external, human nature with frailties and passions

D. The human nature is trumped by the divine nature of the Holy Spirit.
  1. when a person is saved, the Holy Spirit dwells within eternally
  2. when a Christian sins, the Holy Spirit points out the violation of your union with God

E. The flesh has a tendency to take priority over the spiritual.

- Ephesians 5:29, "For no man ever yet <u>hated</u> <u>his own flesh</u>; but <u>nourisheth</u> and <u>cherisheth</u> it, even as the Lord the church."
  1. people spend millions per year on appearance
  2. leisure takes priority over spiritual activities

F. Your strength comes from God in Christ Jesus, so being strong-willed pulls you away, not closer.

- Colossians 2:6-10, "As ye have therefore received Christ Jesus the Lord, <u>so walk ye in him</u>: <u>Rooted and built up in him</u>, and <u>stablished in the faith</u>, as <u>ye have been taught</u>, abounding therein with thanksgiving. Beware lest any man spoil you through philosophy and vain deceit, after the tradition of men, after the rudiments of the world, and not after Christ. For in him dwelleth all the fulness of

the Godhead bodily. And ye are complete in him, which is the head of all principality and power."
1. the sin of unbelief is not letting God lead
2. Jesus is living inside the believer and has all power in heaven and earth

III. Love is the proof.
Love God or self?

A. How can I get close to God and stay there? The Bible tells me to love God above all.

- Matthew 22:37, "Jesus said unto him, Thou shalt love the Lord thy God with all thy heart, and with all thy soul, and with all thy mind."

B. The motives in which we do all things are centered around the fact of our love for God. What is your motive?

1. I want to seek God – to be a better person or to please God
2. commit to Bible study – for God to bless me or to learn more about God
3. memorize and meditate on scripture – to show how spiritual I am or make scripture a part of my thinking to make the right decisions
4. overcome temptations – to build my will or become fruitful for the glory of God
5. fast and pray – to lose weight and have better health or be more receptive to the leading of the Holy Spirit
6. dedicate yourself to God's will – to make up for the past or allow God to work through you in Christ
7. give money – for God to bless my finances or help meet the needs of God's work of the ministry

- I Corinthians 3:13, "Every man's work shall be made manifest: for the day shall declare it, because it shall be revealed by fire; and the fire shall try every man's work of what sort it is."

C. Is it possible to have a relationship with God and still not believe who he is?

- Revelation 2:4, "Nevertheless I have somewhat against thee, because thou hast left thy first love."
  1. the church at Ephesus labored in patience but lacked true love
  2. as the serpent beguiled Eve in the garden of Eden, the slow moving corruption moved this church away from Christ

D. Your love for Christ can grow old as well-meaning as you can be.

- I Corinthians 13:1, "Though I speak with the tongues of men and of angels, and have not charity, I am become as sounding brass, or a tinkling cymbal."

E. How can I keep my love strong and prove my love?

- Romans 8:35, "Who shall separate us from the love of Christ? shall tribulation, or distress, or persecution, or famine, or nakedness, or peril, or sword?"
  1. realize that true love is not of this world
  2. true love comes from God through Jesus Christ

F. God would not accept Cain's offering, but Abel's offering was honored.

- I John 4:10, "Herein is love, not that we loved God, but that he loved us, and sent his Son to be the <u>propitiation</u> for our sins."

    Closer look:
    - ➤ "propitiation," is the Greek word "hilasmos," meaning the "atonement;" reparation, compensation, payment, and restitution
    - ➤ the Lord wants us to accept his love by the cross of Jesus who is our propitiation

G. The clear definition of unbelief is the absence of faith in God, as Paul states:

- Romans 14:23, "...for whatsoever is not of faith is sin."
    1. sin will keep you from loving God
    2. sin of unbelief keeps you from accepting what God offers you
    3. the sin of unbelief rejects faith

TEST YOUR KNOWLEDGE

SECTION X

1. Can a person attend church for many years and not be saved? Yes ___ No ___
2. What is the main reason why a person will not enter into "his rest"?
    a. misunderstanding ___
    b. unbelief ___
    c. unrepentant ___
3. Because of Jesus' finished work on the cross, we can come "_____" unto the throne of grace, according to Hebrews 4:16.
4. Even after salvation, we can battle unbelief that leads to: (list all three)
    a. wasted t_____ (Eph. 5:16)
    b. wasted e_____ (Matt. 13:21)
    c. spiritual s_____ (I Kings 18:21)
5. We can choose a carnal path of the unsaved. True ___ False ___
6. Complete these verses found in Romans 8:6-8 – "For to be _____ _____ is death: but to be _____ _____ is life and peace. Because the carnal mind is _____ _____ God: for it is not subject to the law of God, neither indeed can be. So then they that are in the _____ cannot _____ God."
7. The Spirit always takes priority over the flesh. True ___ False ___
8. According to Matthew 22:37, I am to love God with all my:
    a. heart ___
    b. soul ___
    c. mind ___
    d. all the above ___
9. Your love for God can be judged by your motives to serve him. True ___ False ___

10. Complete this verse found in I Corinthians 3:13 – "Every man's work shall be made _____: for the day shall _____ it, because it shall be _____ by ____; and the fire shall ____ every man's _____ of what sort it is."
11. The church at Ephesus had somewhat of a problem because Jesus declared that they: "L____ thy f_____ l_____."
12. A Christian can grow cold of the love of Christ.
True ___ False ___
13. True love comes from God and is not of this w_____.
14. Who is the only propitiation for our sins? _____ _____
15. The clear definition of "unbelief" is the absence of "_____" in God. (Rom. 14:23)

Take the High Road

Doing the Right Thing

The High Cost of Low Living.

Section XI

- ❖ Making the Right Choices
- ❖ Righteous
- ❖ Judgment
- ❖ Godly Choices

I. Making the right choices.

A. What determines our choices?
    1. the appearances can be attractive
    2. personal gain

- Genesis 13:10, "And Lot lifted up his eyes, and beheld all the plain of Jordan, that it was well watered every where…"

B. Lot chose the city of Sodom. Did he make the right choice?

- Genesis 13:13, "But the men of Sodom were <u>wicked</u> and <u>sinners</u> before the Lord <u>exceedingly</u>."
1. maybe he did not know the culture there of sin city
2. perhaps he just got caught in the wrong place at the wrong time

C. Something was happening to have heavenly visitors show up at Abraham's door.

- Genesis 18:1-2, "And the Lord appeared unto him in the plains of Mamre: and he sat in the tent door in the heat of the day; And he lift up his eyes and looked, and, lo, <u>three men stood by him:</u> and when he saw them, he ran to meet them from the tent door, and <u>bowed himself toward the ground.</u>"

D. The Lord chose to validate the situation first hand.

- Genesis 18:20-22, "And the Lord said, Because the cry of Sodom and Gomorrah is great, and because their <u>sin is very grievous</u>; <u>I will go down now, and see whether they have done altogether according to the cry of it</u>, which is come unto me; and if not, I will know. And the men turned their faces from thence, and went toward Sodom: but Abraham stood yet before the Lord."

E. The decision was made by God to destroy the cities, but Abraham knew that Lot and his family dwelt there.

- Genesis 18:23-24, "And Abraham drew near, and said, Wilt thou also <u>destroy the righteous with the wicked</u>? Peradventure there be fifty righteous within the city: wilt thou also destroy and not <u>spare the place</u> for the fifty righteous that are therein?"

F. What happened to Lot living among the wicked? Why did God appeal to Abraham on this matter and not Lot, seeing that he was the one living in sin?

- Genesis 19:1, "And there came <u>two angels</u> to Sodom at even; and Lot sat in the gate of Sodom: and Lot seeing them rose up to meet them; and he bowed himself with his face toward the ground."

- Proverbs 14:12, "There is a way which seemeth right unto a man, but the end thereof are the ways of death."
  1. Lot was prominent in society; he sat at the gate
  2. he went along with the wicked decisions made by the king

G. Abraham intervened once before when Lot and his family were taken captive when war broke out between four kings against five, and the goods of the cities were stolen.

- Genesis 14:14-16, "And when Abram heard that his brother was taken captive, he armed his trained servants, born in his own house, three hundred and eighteen, and pursued them unto Dan. And he divided himself against them, he and his servants, by night, and smote them, and pursued them unto Hobah, which is on the left hand of Damascus. And he brought back all the goods, and also brought again his brother Lot, and his goods, and the women also, and the people."

H. The King of Sodom wanted to reward Abraham for his rescue victory, but Abraham would have no part of this corrupt people or their wealth.

- Genesis 14:22-23, "And Abram said to the king of Sodom, I have lift up mine hand unto the Lord, the most high God, the possessor of heaven and earth. That I will not take from a thread even to a shoelatchet, and that I will not take any thing that is thine, lest thou shouldest say, I have made Abram rich."

II. Righteous?
How is your testimony?

A. Was Lot considered to be a righteous man? People today refuse to go to church and listen to the gospel, but they claim to be religious.
   1. the saved can live in a perverse lifestyle as Lot
   2. conviction is a light to people in a sinful atmosphere

   - II Peter 2:8, "For that <u>righteous man</u> <u>dwelling among them</u>, in seeing and hearing, <u>vexed his righteous soul</u> from day to day with their unlawful deeds."

B. The two visitors arrived at Lot's house and were determined to abide in the streets all night.

   - Genesis 19:2, "And he said, Behold now, my lords, <u>turn in</u>, <u>I pray you</u>, into your servant's house, and <u>tarry all night</u>, and wash your feet, and ye shall rise up early, and go on your ways. And they said, <u>Nay; but we will abide in the street all night</u>."
   1. what was Lot trying to hide
   2. these men were not on a social visit, but a mission

C. The news traveled fast about Lot's house guests, so the whole town seemed to want to <u>know</u> them.

   Closer look:

   > The Greek word for "know" is "yada," meaning to take or have, recognize, or acquaint.
   > Lot thought it to be wicked

   - Genesis 19:7-8, "And said, I pray you, brethren, do not so <u>wickedly</u>. Behold now, I have two daughters which have not <u>known man</u>; let me, I pray you, <u>bring them out</u> unto you, and <u>do ye to them</u> as is good in your eyes: only unto these men <u>do nothing</u>; for therefore came they under the shadow of my roof."

D. Lot had lost his testimony among this people; they did not hesitate to go as far as to break down his door to get their way. The two men pulled Lot back into the house and confronted the situation.

- Genesis 19:11, "And they <u>smote the men</u> that were at the door of the house with <u>blindness</u>, both small and great: so that they <u>wearied themselves to find the door</u>."

E. Sin will take you farther than you want to go, keep you longer than you want to stay, and cost you more than you want to pay.
1. you can't control the sins of others
2. it is difficult to control your own sinful behavior

- Romans 7:18, "...for to will is present with me; but how to <u>perform</u> that which is good <u>I find not</u>."

III. Judgment.
Time of reckoning.

A. Judgment is inevitable to those who blatantly refuse to acknowledge God and his mercy.

- Isaiah 30:1, "Woe to the <u>rebellious children</u>, saith the Lord, that <u>take counsel</u>, but not of me; and that <u>cover</u> with a covering, <u>but not of my spirit</u>..."

B. God warns and makes the way to follow him.

- Genesis 19:15, "And when the morning arose, then the angels <u>hastened Lot</u>, saying, <u>Arise</u>, <u>take thy wife</u>, and <u>thy two daughters</u>, which are here; <u>lest thou be consumed in the iniquity</u> of the city."
1. God is now pronouncing judgment

2. iniquity will be reckoned (Hos. 8:7)

C. Some will mock God as they did Lot, in unbelief and foolishness.

- Genesis 19:14, "And Lot went out, and spake to his sons in law, which married his daughters, and said, <u>Up get you out of this place</u>; for the Lord will destroy this city. But he <u>seemed as one that mocked</u> unto his sons in law."
  1. One can wonder at this point, why did they think Lot was mocking God also?
  2. This was a serious matter. Why couldn't they believe Lot?

- Galatians 6:7, "Be not deceived; God is not mocked: for whatsoever a man soweth, that shall he also reap."

D. It is hard to give up your old life even if a better hope and safer future presents itself. To linger can be deadly.

- Genesis 19:17, "And it came to pass, when they had brought them forth abroad, that he said, <u>Escape for thy life; look not behind thee, neither stay thou in all the plain</u>; escape to the mountain, lest thou be consumed."
  1. it was hard to leave it all behind
  2. not just property and goods, but lives also

E. Clear instruction or alternate plan? God surely won't care if I add or change his plan a little.

- Genesis 19:19-20, "Behold now, thy servant hath found grace in thy sight, and thou hast magnified thy mercy, which thou hast shewed unto me in saving my life; and <u>I cannot escape to the mountain</u>, lest some evil take me, and I die: Behold now, this city is near to flee unto, and it

is a little one: <u>Oh, let me escape thither,</u> (is it not a little one?) and my soul shall live."
   1. the rebellious nature of Lot is obvious
   2. he is affecting his family with this disobedience and probably not aware of it

F. Judgment has come and there is no chance of reversal. God does get the last word; the judgment is final.

- Genesis 19:24-26, "Then the Lord <u>rained upon Sodom and upon Gomorrah brimstone and fire from the Lord out of heaven</u>; And he overthrew those cities, and all the plain, and all the inhabitants of the cities, and that which grew upon the ground. But his <u>wife looked back</u> from behind him, and she became a <u>pillar of salt</u>."
   1. you cannot bring back the past; move on
   2. Lot's wife disobeyed God by looking back and it cost her life

G. Sinful behavior passed down to the family. Lot's daughters had incestuous desires driven by sinful thoughts and intentions
   1. they schemed to lay with their father
   2. they would excuse this behavior by irrational thinking

- Genesis 19:31-32, "And the firstborn said unto the younger, Our father is old, and there is <u>not a man</u> in the earth to <u>come in unto us</u> after the manner of all the earth: Come, let us make our father drink wine, and <u>we will lie with him</u>, that we may preserve seed of our father."

H. The end result of God's judgment and Lot's disobedience affected the lineage negatively, and not positively in Israel's future.

- Genesis 19:37-38, "And the firstborn bare a son, and called his name <u>Moab</u>: the same is the father of the <u>Moabites</u> unto this day. And the younger, she also bare a son, and called his name <u>Ben-ammi</u>: the same is the father of the children of <u>Ammon</u> unto this day."
  1. the Moabites lived as a separate nation from Israel for a thousand years
  2. the Ammonites were cruel people and mortal enemies of Israel

IV. Godly choices.
Risking by decision.

A. The choices we make in the duration of our lives make a difference on what road we choose to take. The high road is difficult, but the low road is more difficult with adverse consequences.

<u>Abraham on the High Road</u>	<u>Lot on the Low Road</u>
*good pasture land	*property closed in, crime infested
*faithful followers	*nobody would listen, family mocked
*wealthy	*wealth had to be guarded
*peace	*no peace, lived in fear
*faith (not always perfect)	*no sign of faith or prayers
*directed by God	*cities destroyed, lived in mountain
*victorious life	*no victories, lost all
	*daughters bare adversaries

B. Let God set you on the high road. Even the saved make wrong choices as "just" Lot.

- II Peter 2:7-9, "And delivered <u>just Lot</u>, vexed with the <u>filthy conversation of the wicked</u>: (For that righteous man dwelling among them, in seeing and hearing, <u>vexed his righteous soul</u> from day to day with their unlawful deeds;) The Lord knoweth how to deliver the <u>godly out</u>

of temptations, and to reserve the unjust unto the day of judgment to be punished."
1. the Holy Spirit gives instructions to obey
2. temptations can be overcome
3. pray for wisdom to make spiritual choices

THE HIGH COST OF LOW LIVING!

TEST YOUR KNOWLEDGE

SECTION XI

1. When Lot lifted up his eyes to choose where he would take his family and possessions, he:
    a. prayed first for God's wisdom _____
    b. let his family make the choice for him _____
    c. saw well-watered plains _____
2. Sometimes choices are made because of appearances. True _____ False _____
3. Abraham was visited by three heavenly guests. Why did they come?
    a. to bless Abraham and his family _____
    b. to see first hand the wickedness of Sodom and Gomorrah _____
    c. to rescue Lot from danger _____
4. Complete this verse found in Proverbs 14:12 – "There is a _____ which seemeth _____ unto a man, but the _____ thereof are the _____ of _____."
5. Had Abraham in the past helped Lot escape tragedy? Yes _____ No _____
6. After the battle between the kings, in which the King of Sodom was rescued with Lot, the King offered Abraham a reward. Did this reward make Abraham rich? Yes _____ No _____ Why or why not? _____
7. Was Lot considered to be a righteous man? Yes _____ No _____
8. The two angels arrived at Sodom and Gomorrah and Lot introduced them to everyone. True _____ False _____
9. These visitors did not want to go into Lot's house, but stay out in the streets all night. True _____ False _____
10. What did the two angels do to the people of the city?
    a. blessed them _____
    b. blinded them _____
    c. nothing _____

11. Complete this popular saying:
Sin will take you _____ than you want to go, _____ you _____ than you want to stay, and _____ you more than you want to _____.

12. How many people escaped the judgment of Sodom and Gomorrah? _____; Who were they? _____, _____, _____

13. Lot's family did not all escape. Who mocked him and stayed behind to be destroyed by the fires of heaven? s____ in l_____ (assuming there were two other daughters)

14. What happened to Lot's wife and why?
   a. she tried to go back for her belongings ____
   b. she looked back after instructed not to ____
   c. she was too close to the fires and destroyed ____

15. Lot's two remaining daughters were now God-fearing women seeking God's wisdom. True ___ False ___

16. The daughters' ploy was to make Lot drunk and conceive a child. True ___ False ___ Did this work? Yes ___ No ___

17. Lot became an ancestor of what two tribes that became separate and adversaries of Israel? M_____, A_____

18. Lot started off wealthy when he dwelt among Abraham, but now he had literally lost everything. True ___ False ___

19. We know that Lot was aware that he was living in a wicked society because the scripture says in II Peter 2:8 that it "_____ his _____ soul."

20. Wrong choices can sometimes result in the, _____ cost of _____ living.

Take the High Road

Doing the Right Thing

The Sin of Indifference

Section XII

- ❖ Making Light of God's Invitation
- ❖ The Most High
- ❖ A Lesson of Humility

I. Making light of God's invitation.

A. What is indifference? The lack of interest or making light of the situation as Jesus stated in the parable of the marriage of the kingdom. (Matt. 22:2-14)

- Matthew 22:5, "But they made light of it, and went their ways, one to his farm, another to his merchandise."
  Closer look:
  - ➢ "light" in the Greek is the word "Ameleo," meaning, to be careless, or negligent, not regard.
  - ➢ not taking the invitation seriously

B. The world today can be categorized in three ways by indifference:

1. selfish gain – what's in it for me

2. thoughtless waste – taking the goodness of God for granted
3. endless frustration – who live and die on their own terms

C. How can a person reject Jesus Christ and the word of God and expect to live his life in God's will and go to heaven?

- Matthew 22:2-3, "The kingdom of heaven is like unto a <u>certain king, which made a marriage for his son</u>, And sent forth his servants to <u>call them</u> that were bidden to the wedding: and <u>they would not come</u>."

- Matthew 24:12, "And because iniquity shall abound, the love of many shall <u>wax cold</u>."
  1. people today are spiritual but not religious
  2. the emphasis on man has become more important than God

D. God provided the sacrifice for mankind, his own Son on the cross.

- Matthew 22:4-6, "Again, he sent forth other servants, saying, Tell them which are bidden, Behold, I have prepared my dinner: my oxen and my fatlings are killed, and all things are ready: <u>come unto the marriage. But they made light of it</u>, and went their ways, one to his farm, another to his merchandise; And the <u>remnant took his servants, and entreated them spitefully, and slew them</u>."
  1. Israel rejected Jesus Christ as their Messiah
  2. they were extremely against the provision to the point of crucifixion

E. The world today has the same attitude about accepting truth. Belief in God is not the same as accepting his Son as the Savior of the world.

- James 2:19, "...the devils also believe, and tremble."

F. The selfish attitude of gain drives people to fulfill their own desires and gamble eternity away.
   1. you can treat the Christian life recklessly and expect full benefit from the Lord
   2. freedoms today all come at a price from faithful men and women fighting the good fight
   3. we can take God for granted and not be thankful to the point of sinful indifference

- James 4:14-17, "Whereas ye know not what shall be on the <u>morrow</u>. <u>For what is your life</u>? It is even a <u>vapour</u>, that <u>appeareth for a little time</u>, and then <u>vanisheth away</u>. For that ye ought to say, If the <u>Lord will</u>, we shall live, and <u>do this, or that</u>. But now ye <u>rejoice in your boastings</u>: all such rejoicing is <u>evil</u>. Therefore to him that <u>knoweth</u> to do good, and doeth it not, to him it is sin."

II. The most high.
God is the final authority.

A. King Nebuchadnezzar witnessed a miracle after Shadrach, Meshach, and Abednego survived the fiery furnace.

- Daniel 3:26-27, "Then Nebuchadnezzar came near to the mouth of the <u>burning fiery furnace</u>, and spake, and said, Shadrach, Meshach, and Abednego, ye servants of the <u>most high God</u>, <u>come forth,</u> and come hither. Then Shadrach, Meshach, and Abednego, came forth of the midst of the fire. And the princes, governors, and captains, and the king's counsellors, being gathered

together, saw these men, upon whose bodies the fire had no power, nor was an hair of their head singed, neither were their coats changed, nor the smell of fire had passed on them."
   1. no doubt that there was a higher power protecting them
   2. this miracle should have made a believer of all people

B. Did Nebuchadnezzar believe in his heart that God is the most high God after this miracle? He made a decree.

- Daniel 3:29, "Therefore I make a decree, That every people, nation, and language, which speak any thing amiss against the God of Shadrach, Meshach, and Abednego, shall be cut in pieces, and their houses shall be made a dunghill: because there is no other God that can deliver after this sort."
   1. Does the law apply to everyone?
   2. The king served other gods, would monotheism work?

C. King Nebuchadnezzar makes his case to state how powerful he is and how his kingdom is flourishing, when he had a dream with visions that filled him with fear.

- Daniel 4:4-6, "I Nebuchadnezzar was at rest in mine house, and flourishing in my palace: I saw a dream which made me afraid, and the thoughts upon my bed and the visions of my head troubled me. Therefore made I a decree to bring in all the wise men of Babylon before me, that they might make known unto me the interpretation of the dream."

D. Who can interpret the dream? The magicians, soothsayers, and astrologers failed.

- Daniel 4:8-9, "But at the last Daniel came in before me, whose name was Belteshazzar, according to the name of my god, and in whom is the spirit of the holy gods: and before him I told the dream, saying, O Belteshazzar, <u>master of the magicians</u>, because I know that the <u>spirit of the holy gods is in thee</u>, and no secret troubleth thee, tell me the visions of my dream that I have seen, and the interpretation thereof."
    1. when all else fails, go to the Pastor
    2. God might want to get your attention
    3. Why not send in the real Godly man first?
    4. you can't put off the inevitable truth

E. Moses dealt with a stubborn pagan leader that would not "let the people go." This leader will not let the "other gods" go. God's judgment is revealed.
    1. the dream pictured the king as a tree that nurtured all people (Dan. 4:10-12)
    2. this tree was hewn down but the stump remained (13-15)
    3. the king's heart would be changed to a heart of a beast (16-17)

- Daniel 4:20-24, "The tree that thou sawest, which grew, and was strong, whose height reached unto the heaven, and the sight thereof to all the earth; Whose leaves were fair, and the fruit thereof much, and in it was meat for all; under which the beasts of the field dwelt, and upon whose branches the fowls of the heaven had their habitation: <u>It is thou, O king</u>, that art grown and become strong: for thy greatness is grown, and reacheth unto heaven, and thy dominion to the end of the earth. And whereas the king saw a watcher and an holy one coming down from heaven, and saying, <u>Hew the tree down</u>, and destroy it; yet leave the stump of the roots thereof in the earth, even with a band of iron and brass, in the tender grass of the field; and let it be wet with the dew of heaven, and let his portion be with the beasts of the field, till seven times pass over him; This is the interpretation, O king, and this is the decree of the most High, which is come upon my lord the king."

III. A lesson in humility. Whose kingdom is it?

A. How would knowing the future affect today? The king pressed Daniel for the interpretation, but did he believe it?

- Daniel 4:29-30, "At the end of the twelve months he walked in the palace of the kingdom of Babylon. The king spake, and said, Is not this great Babylon, that I have built for the house of the kingdom by the might of my power, and for the honour of my majesty?

- Proverbs 16:18, "Pride goeth before destruction, and an haughty spirit before a fall."

B. The Majesty belongs to the true power and glory.

- Daniel 4:31, "While the word was in the king's mouth, there fell a voice from heaven, saying, O king Nebuchadnezzar, to thee it is spoken; The kingdom is departed from thee."
  1. not "thy" kingdom, but "the" kingdom
  2. the majesty was given to you, but you misused it
  3. God could have let anyone run the kingdom

C. In Noah's day, people didn't believe it would rain. They made light of it and were indifferent to the truth.
  1. the sin of indifference is not of unbelief
  2. the sin of indifference is in reality, a "don't care" attitude stemming from a self-sufficient heart

3. no gratefulness to God for his rich blessings
4. to not believe as the Agnostics, doesn't change anything on spiritual facts about God
5. to ignore sin doesn't make the consequences fade away

- Psalms 14:1, "The fool hath said in his heart, There is no God. They are corrupt, they have done abominable works, there is none that doeth good."

D. A seven year time out has begun. What lesson does God teach a man for seven years when he can't talk back?

- Daniel 4:33, "The <u>same hour was the thing fulfilled upon Nebuchadnezzar: and he was driven from men</u>, and did eat grass as oxen, and his body was wet with the dew of heaven, till his hairs were grown like eagles' feathers, and his nails like birds' claws."
1. what kind of understanding did God give him now
2. only God knows how to break the spirit

- Psalms 51:17, "The sacrifices of God are a broken spirit: a broken and a contrite heart, O God, thou wilt not despise."

E. Lesson learned, God is gracious, and life is restored.

- Daniel 4:34, "And at the end of the days I Nebuchadnezzar <u>lifted up mine eyes unto heaven</u>, and <u>mine understanding returned unto me, and I blessed the most High</u>, and I praised and honoured him that liveth for ever, whose <u>dominion is an everlasting dominion</u>, and his kingdom is from generation to generation."

- Daniel 4:36-37, "At the same time my <u>reason returned unto me</u>; and for the glory of my kingdom, mine honour and brightness returned unto me; and my counsellors and my lords sought unto me; and I was established in my kingdom, and <u>excellent majesty was added unto me</u>. Now I Nebuchadnezzar praise and extol and honour the King of heaven, all whose works are truth, and his ways judgment: and those that walk in pride he is able to abase."

F. The high road means a better relationship with God, which includes:
   1. refusing to lean to your own understanding – Prov. 3:5-6
   2. accept his wisdom and reasoning – I Cor. 3:18-20
   3. get out of your comfort zone, don't conform to your own ways – Rom. 12:2

   - John 15:5, "I am the vine, ye are the branches: He that abideth in me, and I in him, the same bringeth forth much fruit: for without me ye can do nothing."

TEST YOUR KNOWLEDGE

SECTION XII

1. If you are not taking God seriously, you are making what of the situation?
    a. fun ____
    b. light ____
    c. unbelief ____
2. Match each category together with its meaning regarding indifference.
    a. selfish gain   ____ who lives and dies on their own terms
    b. thoughtless waste   ____ taking the goodness of God for granted
    c. endless frustration   ____ "what's in it for me" attitude
3. Is it possible to reject Jesus Christ and God's Word and still go to Heaven? Yes ____ No ____
4. People today are spiritual but not r_____ toward God.
5. Complete this verse found in Matthew 24:12 – "And because _____ shall abound, the love of many shall _____ _____."
6. In the parable of the king's marriage for his son, all invited came joyfully. True ____ False ____
7. The king sent out his servants to invite the people to the wedding, with spite, what did they do to his servants?
    a. lied to them ____
    b. gave them a wedding gift ____
    c. slew them ____
8. List the names of the three servants of God thrown into the fiery furnace. S_____, M_____, A_____
9. God delivered these three without a hint of smoke or fire on them. This in turn prompted the king to do what?
    a. try to kill them again ____
    b. make a decree ____
    c. make these men princes ____

10. Did King Nebuchadnezzar believe that God was the most high in his heart? Yes ___ No ___
11. The king had a dream that none of his magicians, astrologers, or soothsayers could interpret, so he thought of this man with the "s_____ of the h_____ gods" whose name is D_____.
12. What did the vision depict Nebuchadnezzar as being that nurtured all people?
    a. a god ____
    b. a prophet ____
    c. a tree ____
13. Complete this verse found in Daniel 4:31; "While the _____ was in the king's _____, there fell a _____ from _____, saying, O king Nebuchadnezzar, to thee it is _____; the kingdom is _____ from thee."
14. The sin of indifference is in reality, a "don't care" attitude stemming from a s____-s_____ heart.
15. How long was the judgment passed upon Nebuchadnezzar? _____
16. God gave Nebuchadnezzar hairs like eagles' feathers and nails like birds' claws and a heart as a _____.
17. Complete this verse found in Daniel 4:34, "And at the end of the days I Nebuchadnezzar lifted ____ _____ ____ _____ _____, and mine _____ returned unto me, and I _____ the most _____, and I _____ and _____ him that liveth for ever, whose dominion is an _____ dominion, and his kingdom is from generation to generation."

TAKE THE HIGH ROAD
DOING THE RIGHT THING

ANSWER KEY

SECTION I

1. Yes
2. liveth, dieth, live, Lord, Lord,
3. a. your family, d. your country
4. No
5. Hands for charity, Eyes to see his power, lips for testimony
6. True
7. manifest, declare, revealed, fire, sort
8. Isaiah 55:9
9. Salvation
10. b. foolishness
11. Solomon, Ecclesiastes 2:11
12. True
13. fool, night, thy soul shall be required of thee
14. ransom, riches, rebuke
15. Jesus Christ

SECTION II

1. c. he killed a man
2. terms, man, timing
3. True
4. knoweth, doeth it not, sin
5. stagnation no life, right living, right decisions, success in life
6. Yes, blood
7. Yes
8. well, accepted, not well, sin, desire
9. True

10. appointed, once, die, judgment
11. Temptation, Lust, Sin, Death
12. Christ, Savior, II Cor. 5:17,
    start working, James 4:7
    flesh, Rom. 6:6
    word, God, Psa. 119:105
    knowledge, wisdom, Prov. 1:7
    Bible believing, Heb. 10:25
    Holy Spirit, Rom. 12:1-2

SECTION III

1. John
2. lilies, field
3. not, world, not, world, truth, word
4. False
5. d. all the above
6. True
7. Yes
8. liar, denieth, Christ, antichrist, denieth
9. fruit
10. Rapture
11. the year king Uzziah died
12. True
13. an angel brought a live coal from the altar and placed it upon Isaiah's mouth
14. understandeth, perceive, Isaiah
15. Jesus Christ
16. Confess, mouth, Believe, heart, raised, dead

SECTION IV

1. True
2. Yes
3. commitment, alter, doubt, transform

4. apprehended, forgetting, behind, reaching, before, press, high calling
5. False, works, dead
6. sight, faith
7. True
8. wayside, rock, thorns, ground
9. ears, hear
10. light
11. lust, flesh
12. guide, encourage, strengthen

SECTION V

1. good, right, truth
2. Sennacherib, Assyria
3. b. stopped the fountains of waters
4. True
5. sober, vigilant, devil, seeking
6. third, fourth
7. Yes
8. Yes
9. old man, body, sin
10. doubt, fear
11. sent an angel to cut off the enemy
12. Bubonic plague, field mice
13. Eve
14. Ye shall not surely die
15. a. add to God's instruction b. misquoted God's instructions, c. try to resist the serpent
16. d., c., a., b.

SECTION VI

1. body, soul, spirit
2. False
3. spirit, Spirit

4. wretched, deliver, body, death
5. True
6. deceitful, desperately wicked
7. b., a., e., d., c.
8. take, farther, want, make, stay longer, stay, cost, more, pay
9. False
10. Saul, Tarsus
11. c. preaching the word
12. Jesus
13. loveth, chasteneth, scourgeth, reveiveth
14. Esau
15. True
16. imaginations, high thing, exalteth, against, knowledge, captivity, thought, obedience

SECTION VII

1. Yes
2. Yes
3. light, eye, eye, full, light, eye, evil, darkness, great, darkness
4. d. all the above
5. True
6. violation
7. heart, diligence, issues
8. gave in to self, gave in to God
9. conformed, transformed,
10. work your plan
11. fire, burned, burned
12. True
13. Yes
14. communications, good manners
15. love, joy, peace, longsuffering, gentleness, goodness, faith, meekness, temperance

SECTION VIII

1. False
2. True
3. c. they would side with Egypt's enemies and fight against them
4. True
5. Yes
6. fool, heart, God, abominable iniquity, none
7. b. a rock
8. c. 2,000,000
9. Lord, not
10. bowing wall, tottering fence
11. True
12. foundation. God, sure, his, nameth, name
13. John 1:11
14. sword
15. False, findeth, lose, loseth, life, find

SECTION IX

1. Stephen
2. b. the tongue
3. fountain, sweet, bitter
4. heart, diligence, issues
5. bitterness, pride, hatred, anger, covetousness, criticality
6. True
7. Mat. 12:34, Jesus
8. Saul, Tarsus
9. heart
10. True

SECTION X

1. Yes
2. b. unbelief
3. boldly
4. time, efforts, stalemate
5. True
6. carnally minded, spiritually minded, enmity, against, flesh, please
7. False
8. d. all the above
9. True
10. manifest, declare, revealed, fire, try, work
11. left, first love
12. True
13. world
14. Jesus Christ
15. faith

SECTION XI

1. c. saw well watered plains
2. True
3. b. to see first hand the wickedness of Sodom and Gomorrah
4. way, right, end, ways, death
5. Yes
6. No, because he would not accept anything
7. Yes.
8. False
9. True
10. b. blinded them
11. farther, keep, longer, cost, pay
12. 4, Lot, his wife, and two daughters
13. sons, law
14. b. she looked back after instructed not to
15. False

16. True
17. Moabites, Ammonites
18. True
19. vexed, righteous
20. high, low

SECTION XII

1. b. light
2. c., b., a.
3. No
4. religious
5. iniquity, wax, cold
6. False
7. c. slew them
8. Shadrach, Meshach, Abednego
9. b. make a decree
10. No
11. Spirit, holy, Daniel
12. c. a tree
13. word, mouth, voice, heaven, spoken, departed
14. self-sufficient
15. 7 years
16. beast
17. up, mine, eyes, unto, heaven, understanding, blessed, High, praised, honoured, everlasting